DISTRIBUTED
ALGORITHMS
AND PROTOCOLS

DISTRIBUTED ALGORITHMS AND PROTOCOLS

Michel Raynal

Professor of Computer Science
IRISA (INRIA-CNRS, University of Rennes), France

Translated by Jack Howlett, *St Cross College, Oxford*

JOHN WILEY & SONS

Chichester · New York · Brisbane · Toronto · Singapore

Library of Congress Cataloging-in-Publication Data:

Raynal, M.
   Distributed algorithms and protocols.

   (Wiley series in computing)
   Translation of: Algorithmes distribués et protocoles.
   1. Electronic data processing—Distributed processing.
2. Algorithms.   3. Computer network protocols.
I. Title.   II. Series.
QA76.9.D5R385   1988   004'.36   87–25409
ISBN 0 471 91754 0(pbk.)

British Library Cataloguing in Publication Data:

Raynal, Michel
   Distributed algorithms and protocols.—
   (Wiley series in computing).
   1. Parallel processing (Electronic computers)
   2. Algorithms   3. Computer network
   protocols
   I. Title
   005.1   QA76.6

ISBN 0 471 91754 0

Typeset by Photo·graphics, Honiton, Devon.
Printed and bound in Great Britain by Biddles Ltd., Guildford

CONTENTS

PREFACE

The design of algorithms is a fundamental part of information science, as shown by the number of books and papers devoted to this. The great majority of these treat the subject in the context of sequential programming, where the flow of control is always in the same direction and at each step in the calculation a single, unique action is performed. These works are generally concerned with the handling of basic data structures such as trees, lists, graphs, matrices and so on, and with the use of such structures in achieving the desired calculation.

Whilst much has been studied and written about sequential algorithms the same cannot be said for the field of parallelism — characterized by the possibility of several control flows existing simultaneously. Parallelism and the relevant types of algorithm were first considered in connection with computer operating systems, where the design of the system itself required a modular separation into elementary computational activities — the processes — the interactions of which had to be managed. The rise of the 'network' concept, together with advances in programming methodology, has led to the concept of communication becoming a basic tool in the design of parallel algorithms and as a result a new body of algorithmic techniques, based on the exchange of messages between activities, has been developed.

In the field of networks such parallel algorithms are called protocols; they provide the services of information transfer and activity control in a set of processes, executing on physically distinct sites and linked by communication channels, that co-operate to perform some specified application. Some of these protocols have become standardized. In the case of distributed systems these parallel algorithms are called distributed algorithms; here they usually provide the basic functions that are essential to all information systems, mutual exclusion for example, and the control functions that are essential to distributed systems, such as detecting termination of a program made up of distributed partitions or managing duplicated copies of the same set of data. Further, independently of any considerations of networks or systems, algorithms traditionally expressed in sequential form can be reformulated in terms of processes communicating by means of messages. Thus the field of distributed algorithms is very broad; and setting aside all considerations of such things as the hardware on which they are executed and their own intrinsic interest we can say that they are characterized by the relation

distributed algorithm = processes + messages.

This book is devoted to distributed algorithms whose function is one of control, where the word control is used in contrast to computation: the algorithms described are concerned with what may be called system functions, meaning that they do not perform some computation and then finish, but provide a service and are ready to do so again at any instant. The following aspects of control are dealt with:

mutual exclusion and election (distributed)
deadlock (warning and detection, distributed)
termination (of distributed algorithms)
management of information transfers (bi-point and multi-point)
management of duplicated data
problems of gaining consensus

Each of these topics is considered in a separate chapter and in each case there is first an analysis of the problem followed by descriptions of algorithms that will solve it, with proofs of correctness. The texts of the algorithms are given in a uniform manner which is itself algorithmic; this uniformity of style is important because it enables a clear distinction to be made between the formulation of the algorithm and the principles on which it is based. So as to be as self-explanatory as possible the style is what may be called 'event-based'—'the occurrence of such-and-such an event has such-and-such an effect'.

Apart from the first chapter, which lays the foundations, the different chapters can be studied independently of each other; this should ease the approach to the different problems.

The book is addressed to all those who are concerned either with algorithms in general or with parallelism in a distributed context. It will provide the software engineer with a collection of distributed algorithms together with investigations and comparisons, and the teacher with the basis for a course on distributed algorithms and the relevant protocols; whilst students will find in it an introduction to the software techniques of distributed information and an account of the basic principles of algorithms and of the protocols that control their operations.

1

INTRODUCTION TO DISTRIBUTED ALGORITHMS

1 PARALLELISM AND DISTRIBUTION

Technological advances, particularly those producing multiprocessor systems with or without common memory and local area networks, and developments in programming methodology, such as those based on the principle of decomposition into independent parts, are together leading us more and more to view a computer program as a set of parallel processes which, because of their mutual independence, can be executed simultaneously – hence the use of the term parallelism. This independence, however, is generally only relative: the several processes may compete for access to resources such as servers of one kind or another, files or peripherals, which are then called shared resources, or communicate among themselves so as to co-operate in achieving a common goal. This competition and co-operation between processes gives rise to specific problems whose solution requires mechanisms for synchronization and communication respectively; the two are closely interwoven and in fact synchronization can be brought about if there is a communication mechanism, and conversely [CRO 75].

In this book we shall be concerned with the case where the supporting system is physically partitioned or distributed, as for example where the parallel-execution program for some given application has to be run on a network, whether local or wide area [PUJ 83]. The essential characteristic of such support is the absence of a common memory accessible by the different processors on which the different processes are running — meaning, of course,

1

essential from the point of view of whatever algorithm is involved; from other points of view the main interest would be in other important characteristics such as reliability or throughput. The absence of common memory means that the problems of control raised by the synchronization and communication activities cannot be handled by the synchronization and memory access primitive, nor by those of communication that enable the processes to share information.

The consequence of this is that parallel algorithms in a distributed context must involve the concept of *message* and therefore primitives must be defined for the issue and receipt of messages; this is in fact the only mechanism on which we shall rely when defining our algorithms. It is important to realize that the behaviour of a distributed system and communication by messages can always be simulated on a system having a centralized architecture; this can be done at reasonable cost and has the advantage of making the distributed algorithms independent of their physical support. This is not the case if the algorithm has been designed in a centralized context, for whilst it is then possible, by duplicating variables, to simulate a central memory, complicated procedures are needed to manage these variables and the method is seldom used in practice. This sets the general scene for our study; we must look at this scene in a little more detail before defining the concept of distributed algorithms.

2 NETWORKS AND DISTRIBUTED SYSTEMS

2.1 General and local networks

Computer networks have provided the first example of a distributed software and hardware structure; the entities comprising the system are the sites at which the computers are located and the communication system that enables these sites to exchange messages.

The first such networks to appear where the big computer networks with a local operating system at each site together with a communications station by means of which that site could both offer services available at other sites to applications running on its own machinery and make its own services available to the other sites. Effort was always concentrated on specifying the communication system and solving the problems to which this gave rise, these latter concerned mainly with message routing — static or dynamic selection of paths – switching — circuit, packet or message — and flow control. The interested reader could consult some of the specialist works on computer networks [MAC 79, LOR 79, TAN 81a] and on the protocols required [TAN 81b] — these protocols generally relating to servers.

The 'universal' or, as it is usually called, 'open system' aspect of these networks has led on the one hand to the definition of norms for usage by means of standard protocols and on the other to a means for defining and implementing standard networks in terms of 'layers', or levels of abstraction, in particular to the ISO seven-layer standard [ZIM 80]. It has thus become possible to graft some very diverse applications on to such networks, for example videotex [GEC 83]. These developments in the partitioning and implementation of networks and use of the principle of abstraction have gone on in parallel with developments in programming languages involving the ideas of program module [PAR 72] and abstract type [LIS 74], culminating in their integration into the language Ada [ICH 83].

Local area networks, because of their smaller scale and more limited objectives, have given rise to a new view of the idea of a distributed system: here it is no longer a question of providing communication between heterogeneous systems but one of designing a single system that is physically implemented on a number of separate sites that can communicate with one another by means of messages. This presents new problems concerning the distribution of control: once the idea of a distributed system is introduced it becomes necessary to specify its components, that is, the distributed algorithms such as, for example, those that ensure mutual exclusion among the various sites or the consistency of the items in a database distributed over the network.

2.2 Characteristics of distributed systems

In addition to the absence of a common memory and the use of a communication system, distributed systems are characterized by

4

there being no global state visible to an observer at any given instant [LEL 77, COR 81]. The only events that a process can be aware of are those within itself and those relating to the sending or receiving of a message. The event associated with the receipt of a message necessarily occurs after that associated with the issuing of that message, and *a fortiori* after all the events before that; it may therefore be impossible to put an arbitrary pair of events in time order and consequently the perception of this order by an observer is necessarily arbitrary [LAM 78]. All the events occurring within the system could of course be put in strict order by giving the control to a single process, but then one would have a centralized system and the advantages of partitioning would be lost. Distributed systems are dealt with exclusively in [COR 81] and [BOC 83].

2.3 What should be distributed, and why?

There is a variety of reasons for distribution, which we can put into two main classes according as the need is inherent in the problem under consideration itself or only in the implementation and the system on which it is implemented.

Thus it is irrelevant to the user of a database that the items it contains may be geographically dispersed, and he need not be aware of this, but for the designer and implementer of the database this dispersion is an imposed condition and therefore inherent in the problem he has to solve; so for the same distributed algorithm the motivation can differ according to the point of view taken.

Given that there are reasons for a distributed algorithm, what should be distributed? Essentially, the answer is the data, the control or both.

Distributed data
This can be done differently according as there is duplication or partitioning of the data [VER 83]. Duplication means that there is a copy of a data item x, say, at each separate site, say x_1, x_2, ..., x_n, where it is needed by the algorithm. The problem then arises of how to ensure consistency among all these copies, that is, that at every instant $x_1 = x_2 = \ldots = x_n = x$, where x is the 'true' value at that instant of the data item x.

Partitioning of data means that, whilst any item is accessible from any site, the full set is broken into partitions and each partition is held at a stated site. The two methods can of course be combined, with partitioning of the full database and duplication of certain elements; as we shall see, this would require there to be adequate means for ensuring consistency.

Distributed control
Independently of the control mechanisms needed for managing duplicated data it may be necessary to distribute control throughout an algorithm. We speak of distributed control in a set of processes when there is no fixed hierarchical relation among these, that is, there is no master process that exercises general control over the algorithm or the system. However, if the supporting system is such that certain functions can be provided only by certain sites it may be necessary to instal a distributed algorithm to allocate these resources; similarly a decision has to be reached by means of agreement among a group of peer processes.

The need for distributed control is often inherent in the problem in hand; for example if the algorithm must be resilient to failures the possibility of continued working in degraded mode must be provided and this rules out central control.

Thus whatever the architecture of the supporting physical system, the need arises for distributed algorithms, meaning algorithms consisting of separate processes that communicate with one another by exchange of messages. The need for such algorithms has been developed here from a consideration of properties of systems but it can arise in other contexts and a variety of types of distributed algorithm can be envisaged, for example for sorting. This is the general idea of distributed algorithms with which this book is concerned; we now examine the concept in more detail.

3 DISTRIBUTED ALGORITHMS

3.1 Basic elements: processes, communication paths

A distributed algorithm has two basic elements: the processes that receive, manipulate, transform and output data and the links along which these data flow and which form a network having both structural and dynamic properties.

3.1.1 Processes

The general concept of a process enables the idea of activity to be made an abstraction; it has been studied mainly in the literature of information systems, [SHA 74, CRO 75, PES 83], to which the reader is referred for the basis. Here we consider only sequential processes, meaning processes in which there is a single direction for the flow of control. These, in order to act in parallel as a group, must be able to respond to any parallelism in their environment and therefore, as they are sequential by nature, must be given a non-deterministic control structure that enables them to wait for one particular event among a set of possibilities. Such a control structure is offered by languages such as CSP [HOA 78] and Ada [ICH 83] and equally by the languages defined by ISO and CCITT for protocol validation and by PDIL developed at ADI for the same purposes.

We can illustrate this with the Ada language. Consider a process P whose purpose is to provide either of two services $S1$, $S2$ according as they are requested at entry points $P.S1$ or $P.S2$ of P; whilst the possibility of providing the service is governed by condition $C1$ or $C2$ respectively. This means that the service S_i can be provided if and only if it is called for at $P.S_i$ and also C_i is satisfied. This is expressed in Ada as follows:

```
task P is
    entry S1, S2;
end P;
task body P is
    ⟨declaration of variables internal to P⟩
begin
    loop select
        when C1 ⇒ accept S1 do
                            ⟨description of service S1⟩
                        end;
    or when C2 ⇒ accept S2 do
                        ⟨description of service S2⟩
                        end;
        end select;
    end loop;
end P;
```

This is a non-deterministic control structure, allowing P to select either of $S1$ or $S2$ according to the circumstances prevailing when the service is called for.

3.1.2. Structural properties of the links

These are topological in nature and characterize the connectivity of the network. All topologies are possible a priori but some seem to be of more fundamental importance than the others and are adopted for most distributed algorithms. These are as follows.

Ring: each process is aware only of its two immediate neighbours, called for convenience the left and right neighbour respectively. Thus the processes form a ring, said to be uni-directional or bi-directional according as the messages can circulate in one direction only or in either.

Star: there is one particular process P_0 that can communicate with any or all of the others whilst each of the others can communicate only with P_0. This gives a hierarchy among the processes and communication is centralized through P_0.

Tree: This is a generalization of the star topology, extending the hierarchy without any limit in principle. The structure of the set of links can be represented by a tree, each node representing a process that can communicate only with its ancestor and with each of its descendants; a terminal or leaf process can communicate only with its ancestor and the single root process only with its descendants.

Fully connected: every process can communicate with any other; the representation here is as a complete graph, with every node representing a process.

As we have said, most distributed algorithms use one or other of these four structures. This of course refers to the structure of the software: if a fully-connected algorithm has to be implemented on a ring-structured communication network, a layer of software has to be interposed between the two to enable the ring to provide the services required by the complete linking.

3.1.3 Properties of the links

Most distributed algorithms make assumptions about the properties of the software links over which messages can be exchanged; there are a variety of these properties, among which the following are the most frequently encountered.

H1: transmission is made without any duplication of messages

H2: transmission is made without any change to the messages

H3: for transmission between any pair of processes, messages are received in the order in which they were sent – there is no alteration in the sequencing

H4: the delay in delivering a message, though random, is finite; this means that any message is delivered within a finite time of its issue, in other words there is no loss of messages

H5: the delay is bounded, meaning that one can be certain that any message will be delivered within a certain fixed time of its being issued; if in addition messages can be lost then one can be sure that a message not received within this delay has been lost.

Most distributed algorithms make some or all of these assumptions, although some make none of them. As with the structural properties, if the hardware does not satisfy the assumptions made by the algorithm a software layer must be interposed so that the conditions are met.

3.2 Features of distributed algorithms

A distributed algorithm has been defined as a set of processes which, by exchanging messages, co-operate to achieve a common end – performing some desired function or providing some required service. As with sequential algorithms it is important to state a number of properties that these algorithms should have; these can be used to evaluate and compare different algorithms for performing the same function.

3.2.1 Degree of partitioning

An important criterion is the extent to which an algorithm is partitioned, a concept related to the symmetry of the roles played by the different processes. There are several levels of symmetry, for example:

Asymmetry: Every process excecutes a different program text, so no two processes can be interchanged. This is the case, for example, with a 'client and server' algorithm.

Textual symmetry: The texts executed by all processes are identical apart from a reference in each text to the name of the process that executes it, and all the names are different. Thus the processes can behave differently according to different messages received.

Strong symmetry: The texts are identical, there being no reference to process names. Identical or different behaviours are again possible, according to messages received.

Total symmetry: The texts are identical and all processes behave in the same way.

These enable the degree of partitioning of control to be specified: asymmetry represents the lowest and total symmetry the highest. There is a study of the concept of symmetry and its application to the definition of a mutual exclusion algorithm in [BUR 81] and an interesting discussion in [CAR 83, RIC 83] of the symmetry of the behaviour of communicating processes. It is found in practice that most distributed algorithms require different names (effectively numbers) to be given to the different processes, and are designed so that conflicts are resolved by giving the privilege to the message coming from the highest numbered process (cf. the method of time-stamping, Section 4.2.3).

3.2.2 Resilience to failures

The more significant a distributed algorithm is, the more resilient it is to failures of its constituent processes. This is related to the previous feature: if a special role is assigned to a single process, failure of that process can be fatal; but if all processes play the same role an algorithm can be designed that will continue functioning in degraded mode.

3.2.3 Assumptions about the network

Not all algorithms make all the assumptions H1–H5 of Section 3.1.3. Taking into account the function to be performed and the generality of physical support systems available, the most attractive algorithm will be the one that makes the fewest assumptions; that is it will require the least sophisticated environment for its execution.

3.2.4 Traffic generated

For a given function, and all other things being equal, the most attractive algorithm will be the most powerful one; and 'power' can be measured by the number of messages exchanged per unit of time, the density of traffic generated on the communication channels or the waiting time for a response.

3.2.5 Global and local states

A distributed algorithm can be constructed by duplicating a centralized algorithm and adding rules for managing the duplicated variables, in which case every process will benefit from a knowledge of the state of the system as a whole even if it does not need all the information represented by that state. The ability of any process to take decisions without needing a knowledge of the global state can form an evaluation criterion for the algorithm; as well as reducing the number of messages that have to be exchanged this increases the resilience to failures.

3.3 Classifying distributed algorithms

An assessment of the quality of a distributed algorithm can be based on the criteria just listed: it is important to realize that they are not mutually independent. These criteria can be used also as a basis for classifying these algorithms, with each class corresponding to a particular answer to a criterion. A warning is necessary here: in a field of study so recent as that of distributed algorithms a rigid classification should not be imposed too early, for there is a serious risk that this could prove later to be inappropriate.

4 SOME CONCEPTS AND TECHNIQUES

4.1 The approach to design

As with sequential algorithms there are several ways in which the design and production of distributed algorithms can be approached, which can be characterized by situating them in positions relative to two extreme methods.

The first of these extremes is based on the invariants of the problem to be attacked, the processes being defined in such a way that these are conserved at every stage in the construction of the algorithm. This method involves, in effect, developing a proof of correctness simultaneously with the algorithm itself; it is used generally for sequential algorithms [DIJ 76, GRI 81]. If defining the necessary properties becomes too complex, stronger criteria can be used and one speaks of the 'principle of satisfying sufficient conditions' [MER 79].

The other extreme is the empirical approach, in which the algorithm is constructed and then checked for correctness. Because of the lack of tools for deriving programs or algorithms from problem specifications this is the method most commonly used in practice.

4.2 Concepts and techniques

Whatever the design and construction methodology employed, distributed algorithms make use of the standard techniques associated with networks, such as using the acknowledgement of receipt of a message to check that it has been sent, broadcasting values to a group of processes and so on. However, new concepts have arisen that are special to distributed algorithms and new methods have been proposed that take account of these; we now consider three – diffusing computations, circulating token and time stamping.

4.2.1 Diffusing computations

The principle involved here was propsed by Dijkstra and Scholten [DIJ 80]; it is used in certain algorithms whose purpose is to exercise a particular type of control. The processes can be linked by their communication paths in any manner whatsoever, but one process is special in that initially it can only issue messages; further, and initially again, only this process can issue messages, and subsequently any other process can issue a message only if it has received one.

Some distributed algorithms for control, such as detecting the termination of a process or of mutual blocking of two or more processes, apply this principle to the spanning tree of the graph representing the processes and their links. The process associated with the root of the tree plays a special role in this control, the program text for this differing from that of all the others. The principal is used to broadcast an item of information and get the corresponding response, by means of the following sequence of operations:

(a) The root process issues a message to each of its descendants in the spanning tree, this latter representing the topology of the communication paths of the control algorithm.
(b) On receiving the message each node processor re-issues this to each of its descendants and waits for a reply; it then sends a reply to its ancestor in the tree.
(c) If the process referred to in (b) is a leaf process it returns a reply immediately (having no descendants).
(d) The computation ends when the root has received all the replies.

Clearly, if each response in this sequence is merely an acknowledgement of receipt of the message, the effect has been simply to broadcast an item of information throughout a set of processes linked in a tree structure; but the response can, if wished, carry much more information, in which case the diffusing computation can become a very powerful technique, as illustrated in the discussion of termination algorithms in Chapter 4.

4.2.2 Circulating token

The 'token' here is a privilege or priority that is made to circulate around a set of processes connected in a ring structure; as before, the ring can either be specified statically or be reconfigured dynamically. This technique, which is important on account of its conceptual simplicity, is used particularly by algorithms for termination and mutual exclusion.

4.2.3 Time stamping

The principle here, due to Lamport [LAM 78], is used in many distributed algorithms in which choices have to be made in an equitable manner; this is particularly the case for algorithms that enter into distributed systems, such as those for mutual exclusion and detection of mutual blocking. A conflict must not be resolved every time by choosing the same process, for this could risk starving the others. The risk is avoided in central systems by recourse to the central memory or to the global system clock, but these are not available in a distributed system; to overcome this difficulty, and consequently to enable an order to be established among the events with which the system is concerned, Lamport proposes the principle of time stamping, called also the principle of logical clocks.

Each process or site P_i owns and manages a logical clock h_i, used to define a measure of local time; h_i is an integer variable, initialized to 0, whose successive values form a strictly increasing sequence. Every message m issued by P_i is stamped with the current value of h_i and with the number of the process, giving the triplet (m, h_i, i).

The mechanism of the time-stamping method causes the process P_i to manage its clock h_i as follows:

(a) When P_i receives a message (m, h_j, j) it sets h_i to the value $[\max (h_i, h_j) + 1]$ which is then taken as the time at which the message was received. This clearly avoids any problems of drift among the various clocks of the communicating processes.

(b) When P_i issues a message (m, h_i, i) the value of h_i is incremented before including in the message, and this incremented value is taken as the time of issue of the message.

(c) The logical clock h_i can also be incremented between pairs of events internal to P_i, but this is unnecessary if one is interested only in the communication.

This mechanism makes it possible to label the events in a consistent manner in relation to the interactions between the processes, that is, the issue and receipt of messages: in terms of time as defined by the logical clocks, an issue will always precede the corresponding receipt. Thus the mechanism provides an ordering among the events; but this is only a partial ordering because two independent events – that is events not linked either directly or indirectly by some causal relation – can be stamped with the same logical time. If, for reasons of equitability for example, a total order is needed by the algorithm it is always possible to derive this from the partial ordering by means of a topological sort.

The number i of the process P_i, transmitted with every message issued by P_i, is used by Lamport's method to resolve any conflicts. In the total ordering the message (m, h_i, i) is considered as preceding (m', h_j, j) if and only if

(a) $h_i < h_j$: the issue of m precedes that of m' in the logical clock system and the relations of precedence that this entails; or

(b) $h_i = h_j$ and $i < j$: m and m' are issued at the same logical time, so the corresponding events are not ordered in this system; the numbers of the issuing processes are therefore used to decide an order.

Thus the method makes the specification of each process's identity form part of its program text; so the situation is in effect that of textual symmetry defined in Section 3.2.1, where the only difference between the program texts is in the name of the process.

4.3 Communication + ordering = control

By its very definition, a distributed algorithm is based on communication of messages. What we have been discussing shows that in very many cases this communication can take place according to a particular topology — logical ring, tree structure — and with the use of a particular technique — circulating token, diffusing computation. Thus there is a relation of appropriateness between the structures of the topology and of the communication control, just as there is in sequential algorithms between data structure and control — arrays and iteration, lists and recursivity for example; and as our subject is so new, other important relations will certainly become evident. It is important to remember that ring and tree structures are essentially dynamic: they can be reconfigured and, provided that they do not fix the graph of the communication paths once and for all, can involve at any time only a subset of this full set.

Another important aspect, seen in algorithms whose purpose is to control other processes such as detection of mutual blocking or ensuring consistency of distributed data, is the need to ensure equitability in some sense. Several methods are available for meeting this need, all depending on some way of establishing an order among the relevant events, among which time-stamping is the most widely used at present. There are other methods, differing according to the instant at which the ordering is established, so the names 'a priori' and 'a posteriori' methods are given; these methods are used mostly for control of distributed databases [BOK 84].

Each of the following chapters is devoted to a particular problem encountered in connection with distributed algorithms. Processes forming parts of algorithms are expressed in a Pascal-like language, for both control and data structures. When discussing control structures whose behaviour can be non-deterministic we have used the term 'event-driven' in connection with handling of certain events in a process, such as receipt of messages or checking that a condition holds; such activities are executed as atomic processes, that is, as non-interruptible processes, with the exception of the primitive WAIT (C), which allows a process to wait until condition C is satisfied.

REFERENCES

[BOC 83] BOCHMANN, G. V., *Concepts for Distributed Systems Design*, Springer Verlag (1983).

[BOK 84] BOKSENBAUM, C., CART, M., FERRIE, J. and PONS, J. F., *Le contrôle de cohérence dans les Bases de Données Réparties*. RR 17, CRIM, Université de Montpellier (Nov. 1984), 30 p.

[BUR 81] BURNS, J.E., Symmetry in Systems of Asynchronous Processes, *Proc. 22nd Annual Symposium on Foundations of Computer Science* (Oct. 1981), pp. 169–174.

[CAR 83] CARVALHO, O., and ROUCAIROL, G., On Mutual Exclusion on Computer Networks, *Comm. ACM*, **26**(2), (Feb. 1983), pp. 146–147.

[COR 81] CORNAFION (group name), *Systèmes Informatiques Répartis*, Dunod (1981), 368 p.

[CRO 75] CROCUS (group name), *Systèmes d'Exploitation des Ordinateurs*, Dunod (1975), 364 p.

16

[DIJ 76]   DIJKSTRA, E. W., *A Discipline of Programming*, Prentice-Hall (1976).

[DIJ 80]   DIJKSTRA, E. W., and SCHOLTEN, C. S., Termination Detection for Diffusing Computations, *Inf. Proc. Letters*, 11(1) (Aug. 1980), p. 1–4).

[GEC 83]   GECSEI, J., *The Architecture of Videotex Systems*, Prentice-Hall (1983), 276 p.

[GRI 81]   GRIES, D., *The Science of Programming*, Springer Verlag (1981), 366 p.

[HOA 78]   HOARE, C. A. R., Communicating Sequential Processes, *Comm. ACM*, 21(8) (Aug. 1978), pp. 666–677.

[ICH 83]   ICHBIAH, J. *et al.*, Reference Manual for the ADA Programming Language, *ANSI/MIL-STD 1815 A* (Jan. 1983).

[LAM 78]   LAMPORT, L., Time, Clocks and the Ordering of Events in a Distributed System, *Comm. ACM*, 21(7) (July 1978), pp. 558–565.

[LEL 77]   LELANN, G., Distributed Systems: Towards a Formal Approach, *IFIP Congress, Toronto* (Aug. 1977), pp. 155–160.

[LIS 74]   LISKOV, B., and ZILLES, S., Programming with Abstract Data Types, *Proc. ACM-Sigplan Conf. on VHLL, Sigplan Notices*, 9(4) (1974), pp. 52–59.

[LOR 79]   LORRAINS (group name), *Réseaux Téléinformatiques*, Hachette (1979).

[MAC 79]   MACCHI, C., and GUILBERT, J. F., *Téléinformatique*, Dunod (1979), 642 p.

[MER 79]   MERLIN, P. M., Specification and Validation of Protocols, *IEEE Trans. on Comm.*, 27(11) (Nov. 1979), pp. 1671–1680.

[PAR 72]   PARNAS, D. L., A Technique for Software Module Specification with Examples, *Comm. ACM*, 15(5) (May 1972), pp. 330–336.

[PES 83]   PETERSON, J. L., and SILBERSCHATZ, A., *Operating Systems Concepts*, Addison Wesley (1983), 548 p.

[PUJ 83]   PUJOLLE, G., *Les réseaux d'Entreprises*, Eyrolles (1983), 149 p.

[RIC 83]   RICART, G., and AGRAWALA, K., Author's response to 'On Mutual Exclusion in Computer Networks' by Carvalho and Roucairol, *Comm. ACM*, 26(2) (Feb. 1983), pp. 147–148.

[SHA 74]   SHAW, A., *The Logical Design of Operating Systems*, Prentice-Hall (1974), 306 p.

[TAN 81a] TANENBAUM, A. S., *Computer Networks*, Prentice-Hall (1981), 517 p.

[TAN 81b] TANENBAUM, A. S., Networks Protocols, *Computing Surveys* (Dec. 1981), pp. 453–489.

[VER 83]   VERJUS, J. P., Synchronisation in Distributed Systems: an
            Informal Introduction, in *Distributed Computing Systems*,
            Academic Press (1983), pp. 3–22.
[ZIM 80]   ZIMMERMANN, H., OSI Reference Model – the ISO Model
            of Architecture for open Systems Interconnection, *IEEE
            Trans. on Comm.*, **28** (Apr. 1980), pp. 425–432.

2

ELECTION AND MUTUAL EXCLUSION ALGORITHMS

1 INTRODUCTION

A problem that often arises in connection with communicating processes that co-operate to achieve a common goal is that of deciding, at any given instant, to which of the processes a particular privilege should be assigned. The requirement can take either of two forms according to the nature of the goal:

(a) bringing about a mutual exclusion, when the choice of the privileged process must be made equitably and that process must not hold the privilege for an indefinite period;
(b) election by all the processes of one to which the privilege shall be assigned permanently.

We study these two aspects of the problem in this chapter.

2 THE MUTUAL EXCLUSION PROBLEM

This is one of the first problems met in parallel programming: the several processes, operating in parallel, compete for resources that cannot be shared and therefore constraints have to be applied to ensure that when one process is using such a resource none of the others can gain access to it. The first software solution to this problem of mutual exclusion was due to Dekker [DIJ 65] and used only the primitive operations of reading and writing a word in memory; many more have been proposed since then, differing in their properties (e.g. equitable or not) and in the number and the nature of the variables they need.

In a distributed system the specification of a mutual exclusion algorithm cannot be made to depend on access to central memory but must be in terms of message exchanges; the protocol must provide both equitability and freedom from mutual blocking, that is, any process that wishes to enter the critical section must be able to do so within a finite time.

In an earlier book [RAY 86] I have dealt exclusively with this problem and its solution and a number of algorithms are given. We must recall here the distinction made between distributed algorithms based on the use of state variables (such a variable being 'distributed' in the sense that at any instant it can be read by any process but written to by only a designated one) and those based on communication of messages. The activities involving the distributed variables of the algorithms of the first class can of course be expressed in terms of the sending and receiving of messages, but the effect of this is to mix the logic of the algorithm with that of its implementation, and consequently to obscure the presentation and make understanding more difficult. Such algorithms therefore are best suited to distributing control in a centralized architecture, resulting in reliable algorithms that are resilient to failures — properties not possessed by centralized algorithms.

We shall study here distributed algorithms based on messages. [RAY 86] gives a number of these: Lamport's algorithm [LAM 78] which uses a distributed queue, a full account of which is given in [PLO 84], in Ada; Lelann's [LEL 77], using a token circulating round a ring; Ricart and Agrawala's [RIC 81], which aims to minimize the number of messages; and that of Carvallo and Roucairol [CAR 83] which also seeks to minimize the number of messages but uses a different definition of symmetry. We shall not deal with these but will give a mutual exclusion algorithm that is described in two separate publications ([RIC 83] and [SUZ 82]); its importance is that it needs only n messages or none at all to bring about the desired exclusion in a set of n processes.

3 THE RICART AND AGRAWALA/SUZUKI KASAMI ALGORITHM

3.1 Overview of other algorithms

Lamport's algorithm [LAM 78] needs $3(n - 1)$ messages to ensure mutual exclusion in a set of n processes: $n-1$ each for distributing the request for access to the critical section by one of the processes, for conveying the agreement to this of the other $(n-1)$ and for broadcasting the news when the critical section becomes free again. Ricart and Agrawala's algorithm [RIC 81] needs only $2(n - 1)$; $n-1$ for a process P_i to inform the others of its wish to enter the critical section, and $n-1$ for conveying the agreements, as before; no explicit messages are sent to say that this section is free, any process that was using it being deemed to have released it when agreeing to its use by another. Carvallo and Roucairol's algorithm [CAR 83] can need any number between zero and $2(n - 1)$, using a different definition of symmetry to optimize Ricart and Agrawala's [CAR 83, RIC 83]: if a process P_i has used the critical section and asks for access again after a period during which no other process has asked for access, then P_i considers that it has permanent access and does not make a further request when it next needs access; this enables the number of messages to be reduced.

All these algorithms ensure the desired exclusion, are equitable and prevent mutual blocking by the processes; the equitability results from the use of time-stamping, which enables an ordering to be established among the messages and any conflicts to be resolved. All these properties are discussed by Raynal [RAY 86].

3.2 Assumptions

We now describe the algorithm devised by Ricart and Agrawala as a result of their attempt to reduce the number of messages needed. It makes the following assumptions about the communication network:

(a) The network is fully linked.
(b) The transmission is error-free.

(c) The delay is variable.

(d) Desequencing is possible — i.e. messages may be received in an order different from that in which they were sent.

3.3 Principles of the algorithm

The privilege that allows a process to enter the critical section is represented by a *token*, which must be held by any process using this section; and any process that holds the token can enter this section without requesting permission of the other processes (cf. [CAR 83]). Initially the token is assigned arbitrarily to one of the processes; a process P_i $(i = 1,2 \ldots, n)$ that wishes to use the critical section will not know which of the other processes holds the token at that instant and will request it by issuing a message that is time-stamped and broadcast to all the others. The essential difference between this algorithm and those just described lies in the definition and implementation of the token: this takes the form of an object manipulated by the processes, consisting of an array whose kth element records the time-stamp of the last time it was assigned to the process P_k. When the process holding the token, P_j say, no longer needs to use the critical section it searches this array in the order $j+1$, $j+2$, $\ldots$, n, 1, 2, $\ldots$, $j-1$ for the first value of l such that the time-stamp of P_l's last request for the token is greater than the value recorded in the token for the time-stamp of P_l's last holding of the token. P_j then transfers the token to P_l.

3.4 The algorithm

The following variables are declared in each process P_i:

```
clock:          0, 1, . . .    initialized 0;    (logical clock)
token_present:  boolean;
token_held:     boolean initialize F;
token:          array (1, 2, . . ., n) of (0, 1, . . .) initialized 0;
requests:       array (1, 2, . . ., n) of (0, 1, . . .) initialized 0;
```

The boolean 'token_present' is initialized to F (false) in every process except one, this one holding the token at the start; the texts of all the processes are identical at the start, each identified as i.

The operation **wait** (access, token) causes the process to wait until a message of the type 'access' is received, which is then put into the variable 'token'; after such a wait other request messages can be received and processed.

The algorithm is in two parts; the first part deals with the use of the critical section and consists of a prelude, followed by the critical section and ending with a postlude, the second part deals with the actions to be performed when messages are received. The texts are as follows, where the notation is that of [RAY 86].

```
if ¬ token_present then begin clock ← clock + 1;              [Prelude]
                            broadcast (requests, clock, i);
                            wait (access, token);
                            token_present ← T;
                      end;
end if;
token_held ← T;
    ⟨critical section⟩
token (i) ← clock;                                           [Postlude]
token_held ← F;
for j from i+1 to n, 1 to i−1 do
                      if request (j) > token (j) ∧ token_present then
     begin token_present ← F:
        send (access, token) j;
                      end;
                  end if;

when received (request, k, j) do
                  request (j) ← max(request (j), k);
                  if token_present ∧ ¬ token_held then
                      ⟨text of postlude⟩
                      end if;
end do;
```

Notes: 1. If the token is not present, the prelude consists in broadcasting the request to all the other processes and waits until the token arrives.

2. The postlude first records in the token the time of its last holding by P_i, looks to see if any process has requested the token and if so transfers it appropriately.

3. The receipt of a request from P_j has the effect of updating the local variable 'request (j)' which records the time of P_j's last request, followed by the transfer of the token if it is neither held nor being used by any other process.

3.5 Proof of the algorithm

Mutual exclusion
Proving that this is ensured is equivalent to showing that at any one time the maximum number of variables token_present that can have the value T (true) is 1; and since this is the initial value it suffices to show that the value is conserved throughout the procedure.

Consider first the prelude. The variable for P_i, which we write token_present$_i$, changes its value from F to T when P_i receives the token. If we now consider the postlude for the process P_j that has issued the token, we see that P_j has been able to do so only if token_present $_j$ had the value T and P_j had changed this to F before sending the token. This establishes the exclusion property.

Notice that all the token_present variables have the value F when and only when the token is in the process of being transferred.

Fairness and absence of deadlock
The absence of deadlock can be established by a *reductio ad absurdum* argument. Suppose that all the processes wish to enter the critical section but none of them has the token, so they are all halted, awaiting its arrival. The token is therefore in transit, it will after some finite time arrive at one of the processes (recall that, by hypothesis, the transmission delay is variable and desequencing is possible) and so unblock it.

The fairness follows from the fact that all messages are delivered within a finite time of issue. The postlude requires that P_i transfers the token to the first process P_l, found in scanning the set in the order $l=i+1, i+2, \ldots, n, 1, \ldots, i-1$, whose request has reached P_i; if the transmission delays for all messages are finite (i.e. no message is lost) all the processes will learn of the wish of some P_j to enter the critical section and will agree to this when its turn comes.

3.6 Messages and time-stamping

Number and size of messages

The algorithm requires either n messages ($n-1$ to broadcast the request and 1 to transfer the token) when the requesting process does not already hold the token, or 0 when it does.

The messages are of two types, the requests and the token itself. Those of the first type consist of three elements: one defines the type, one the value of the clock and one the identity of the process. Those of the second type have $n+1$ elements: the type and n clock values. Notwithstanding the large size of the messages of type 'token', this algorithm is preferable, so far as the number of messages needed is concerned, to the others mentioned.

Use of time-stamping

In this algorithm the time-stampings of the request messages are not used, as they are in Lamport's, to reset the clocks and so correct any drifts; they are used simply as counters that record the number of times the various processes have asked to use the critical section, and so to find whether or not the number of times that P_i has been given this access, recorded as the value of token(i), is less than the number of requests it has made, known to P_j by the value of request$_j(i)$. The function 'max', used in the processing associated with the reception of requests, results in only the last request from P_j being considered if several had been delivered out of sequence.

If the additional assumption has to be made that messages can be lost, two problems arise. If the lost message is a request, then, unless there is a recovery procedure based on a time-out mechanism, the process making the request is removed from the competition for the critical section and is halted, no longer able to access this; in this case the algorithm continues to operate as before but with only the remaining processes. But if the loss is of the message conveying the token, the algorithm loses many of its properties: mutual exclusion is maintained but deadlock begins to appear. This last problem also arises if the process holding the token fails; we now study a distributed algorithm for regenerating a lost token.

4 AN ALGORITHM FOR REGENERATING THE TOKEN

4.1 A token circulating on a logical ring

There is an exceedingly simple algorithm for mutual exclusion when the topology of the communication between processes is that of a ring, meaning that each process can communicate only with one of its neighbours or with both, according as the ring is unidirectional or bidirectional. Again, the privilege is represented by a special message, the token, which the processes hand from one to the other around the ring, so the protocol controlling the use of the critical section by the process P_i (i in 0, 1, . . ., $n-1$ for n processes) is as follows.

```
wait (token) of P_{(i-1)mod n};
  ⟨critical section⟩
send (token) P_{(i+1)mod n};
```

This algorithm ensures mutual exclusion because there is only one message of the type 'token'; further, if the ring is unidirectional there can be neither deadlock nor starving, as the token circulates from process to process around the ring.

However, problems can arise concerning resilience to failures, and these are of two sorts, those resulting from the failure of a process and those from loss of the token. The first are dealt with by identifying the failed process and reconfiguring the ring; methods, based on the principle of 'mutual distrust', are described in [LEL 77] and [COR 81]. Here we consider the loss and regeneration of the token.

4.2 Loss of token: Misra's algorithm

The usual methods for detecting the loss of the token and setting in motion the actions needed to recover from this loss are described in [LEL 77] and [PES 83] – the 'bully algorithm'; these involve use of the time-outs, and require the identities of the individual processes to be known. The reason for this last requirement is that if the delays are not measured accurately enough a lost token can be regenerated by several processes but only one copy must be retained; the identities, all of which are different, are used to bring this about.

Misra [MIS 83] has proposed a method that requires knowledge neither of delays nor of process identities. It uses two tokens, each of which serves to detect the possible loss of the other, by this means: a token T1 arriving at the process P_i can guarantee that the other token T2 has been lost — and can therefore regenerate it — if neither it nor P_i has encountered T2 since T1's last passage through P_i. Whilst the behaviours of the two tokens are symmetrical, the privilege with which the mutual exclusion is concerned is, of course, associated with only one.

The loss of a token is detected by the other in one passage round the ring; and the algorithm works only when one token having been lost, the other makes a complete turn round the ring without itself being lost. To deal with this possibility the algorithm can be generalized to use any number of tokens, when it will work so long as one remains on the ring.

The algorithm

Let us call the tokens 'ping' and 'pong', and with these associate numbers 'nbping', 'nbpong' respectively, equal in absolute value but opposite in sign, that record the number of times the tokens have met; these numbers are therefore related by the constraint

$$nbping + nbpong = 0$$

Initially the two tokens are both in an arbitrarily chosen process and the values are

$$nbping = 1, \; nbpong = -1$$

Each process P_i carries an integer variable m_i, initialized to 0, that records the number, nbping or nbpong, associated with the token that last passed through P_i. The behaviour of P_i as follows.

```
when received (ping, nbping) do
            if m_i = nbping then
                begin ⟨pong is lost, regenerate it⟩
                        nbping ← nbping + 1;
                        nbpong ← −nbping;
                end;
                else m_i ← nbping;
            end if;
            end do;
when received (pong, nbpong) do
                ⟨as before, interchanging ping and pong⟩
            end do;
when meeting (ping, pong) do
                nbping ← nbping + 1;
                nbpong ← nbpong − 1;
            end do;
```

Essentially, the algorithm conserves the relation nbping + nbpong = 0, changing these numbers appropriately each time the tokens meet. When P_i receives one of the tokens it compares m_i with the associated number. Suppose this is nbping and $m_i \neq$ nbping; then either m_i has been changed since the last passage of ping, meaning that pong has passed through P_i in the meantime, or the two tokens have met and consequently their numbers have been changed to record this: the passage of ping is then recorded by P_i setting $m_i := $ nbping. If P_i finds that $m_i = $ nbping then pong was not the last token to pass through P_i (for otherwise m_i would have been modified appropriately and the negative values recognized by P_i) nor have the tokens met in their passage round the ring (for then nbping would have been increased by 1 to record the fact). Therefore pong must have been lost and P_i can regenerate it, setting the values of nbping and nbpong appropriately.

Values of nbping, nbpong

As the procedure has been described, there is no limit in principle to these counter values, and this would constitute a major disadvantage of the algorithm. They can, however, be bounded, by a device that requires only comparisons of the equal/unequal type and no greater than/less than discrimination, and therefore a simple hardware implementation.

Suppose there are n processes P_i. When the counters are updated, as a result either of meeting or of one having been lost and regenerated, their absolute values must be different from all the values m_i. It is thus sufficient to increment them modulo $(n+1)$:

nbping, for example, cannot then have the same value as any of m_i, for this could result only from its having been updated $n+1$ times since ping's previous passage through P_i, which is impossible since there are only n processes and the tokens meet only once in a process.

5 ELECTIVE ALGORITHMS

5.1 Introduction

From the point of view of control, many algorithms that are called distributed are in fact centralized: there is a single co-ordinating process that performs certain functions on behalf of the others when they ask for these — the classical 'client/server' protocol. Any algorithm for which a centralized expression is known can be implemented thus — mutual exclusion, detection of mutual blocking, etc. — with the messages serving only to convey the requests for service and the results obtained; so far as the using process is concerned everything has the appearance of a call to a distant procedure.

Such an algorithm, like any centralized algorithm or indeed any algorithm for which the texts of its processes are not symmetrical, suffers from the great disadvantage that a failure of the co-ordinating process results in the failure of the algorithm as a whole. This can be overcome by the remaining processes conducting a negotiation among themselves with the aim of electing one of their number to take over the role of co-ordinator. The protocols associated with such negotiations are called elective algorithms. These are usually based on the assumption that each process has a unique identifier, taking the form of a number; if the convention is adopted that at any instance the co-ordinating process is the one with the largest identifier (or alternatively, the smallest), then after a failure of this process the elective protocol consists in choosing the process with the largest (or smallest) of the remaining numbers.

Elective protocols can be useful in distributed algorithms in which one process plays a role that is not necessarily that of co-ordinator but is special in some other way (cf. Dijkstra's algorithm for mutual exclusion [DIJ 74]).

There are several elective algorithms. Two which we shall not describe here are given in [PES 83]: the 'bully algorithm' and an algorithm for ring topology due to Lelann [LEL 77]; if there are n processes each of these algorithms requires n^2 messages for the election. We shall give three algorithms, all assuming ring topology; the first is distinguished by its simplicity and by its methodology – it uses the principle of 'selective extinction' – and the others by requiring only $O(n \log n)$ messages.

5.2 The Chang and Roberts algorithm [CHA 79]

This applies to the case where the processes, the total number of which is not necessarily known, are linked in a unidirectional ring; as above, each process P_i has a unique numerical identifier. The principle is simply one of finding the maximum of a set of numbers asociated with the processes.

The processes can be arranged in any order around the ring. Each process P_i 'knows' the value of its own identifier i, which it transmits to its neighbour on the left, Pj say. P_j then compares this with its own identifier j and transmits the greater to its left-hand neighbour: this is the 'selective extinction' method. The election starts with one process sending such a message and marking itself as taking part in the election – at this stage it will be the only one so marked. The unmarked process receiving the message will act as just described and mark itself as a participant. When a marked (i.e. participating) process receives its own identifier it knows that this must be the greatest and that therefore it is elected to play the special role; and if this is necessary to the working of the algorithm for which the election is being conducted, it must then transmit its identity to all the other processes.

The algorithm
Each process P_i carries the following declarations.

    constant my_number: **value** i;
    variables participant: **boolean initialized** F;
         co-ordinator: **integer**;

The variable 'co-ordinator' is used only if it is necessary for all the processes to know which has been elected.

The messages circulating around the ring are of two types: 'election', indicating that the value transmitted with the message is a candidate for election; and 'elected', indicating that the value is the identifier of the elected process. When 'co-ordinator' is not used, neither are these latter messages (which are used to update the variables). The communication primitive **sendL**, used here, is tailored to the particular ring of processes; it enables a process to send a message to the process designated as its neighbour on the left.

```
when decision (initiate_election) do
                participant ← T;
                sendL (election, my_number);
                end do;
when received (election, j) do
                case j > my_number then begin
                                sendL (election, j);
                                participant ← T;
                                end case;
                    case j < my_number and participant then begin
                                        sendL (election, my_number);
                                        participant ← T;
                                        end case;
                    case j = my_number then sendL (elected, i);
                                end case;
when received (elected, j) do
                co-ordinator ← j;
                participant ← F;
                if j ≠ my_number then sendL (elected, j);
                end if;
        end do;
```

The principle of selective extinction is applied when a process, P_i say, a participant in the election, receives a message from another participant carrying a number less than its own: P_i transmits no message on this occasion, so the received message is 'extinguished' and by continuation all the messages.

Proof of validity of the algorithm
What has to be shown is that the algorithm picks out one and only one number, the maximum.

Because of the unidirectional nature of the ring, a message issued by any process must be received by each of the others before returning to its sender. Only the message carrying the greatest number, once this has been issued, will not be replaced by one carrying a different (greater) number at any stage and only this, therefore, can make a complete circuit of the ring. This message must make a complete circuit because either the corresponding process P_{max} is the one that started the election and therefore issued this message, or it was not the initiator but then would receive a message at some later stage, in response to which it would issue the message carrying this greatest number.

Timing

There are two extreme cases. In the first, every process initiates an election at the same time, with the result that the largest number is found in one turn round the ring; in this case the time required is proportional to the number n of processes. At the other extreme, only the left-hand neighbour of P_{max} initiates the election; the message has then to travel through $n - 1$ processes before reaching P_{max} which then issues the largest number, which in turn has to travel through $n - 1$ processes before returning to P_{max}; so this case requires a time proportional to $2(n - 1)$. In either case, and therefore in general, the time required is $0(n)$.

Number of messages of type 'election'

The most favourable situation is that in which the processes are arranged round the ring in increasing order of their identifying numbers and the election is initiated by P_{max}. The message has then to undergo n transfers before returning to P_{max}, so the number involved here is $0(n)$.

In the least favourable situation the processes are arranged in decreasing order and all initiate an election simultaneously; then the message issued by P_i undergoes i transfers, so the total number is

$$\sum_{i=1}^{n} i = \tfrac{1}{2}n(n + 1)$$

Thus the maximum number of messages is $0(n^2)$.

To deal with the cases intermediate between these we use the fact that the probability $P(i,k)$ that the message i is transferred k times is the probability that the first $k-1$ left-hand neighbours of P_i have identifiers that are less than i and that that of the kth is greater. If we write $C(a,b)$ for the number of combinations of b items from a set of a this is

$$P(i,k) = \frac{C(i-1, k-1)}{C(n-1, k-1)} \times \frac{n-i}{n-k}$$

The message carrying the number n is transferred n times; the mean number of transfers from that of number i is

$$E_i = \sum_{k=1}^{n-1} k\, P(i,k)$$

and therefore the mean total number is

$$E = n + \sum_{i=1}^{n-1} E_i$$

which can be shown [CHA 79] to be $0\,(n \log n)$.

5.3 The Hirschberg and Sinclair algorithm (HIR 80]

This makes a number of the assumptions of the previous algorithm: each process has a unique numerical identifier and is not necessarily aware of the total number of processes; the processes are arranged around a ring in arbitrary order, but now the ring is bidirectional, so that messages can circulate in either direction. The communication primitives are as follows, all relating to a typical process P_i:

sendLR send the same message to both the left-hand and right-hand neighbour

pass pass the message received from the right-hand neighbour to the left (or conversely) without modification

respond send a response to the neighbour from which a message has just been received

These are closely tied to the topology of the bidirectional ring; they could all be expressed in terms of a single primitive **send**, but this would confuse the internal logic of the algorithm with that of the communication system; so we shall prefer to keep to the higher level forms.

The algorithm is based on the idea of conducting a sequence of elections on increasingly large subsets of the processes until all have been included. If P_i initiates an election it declares itself a candidate and seeks to find if its own identifier (whose value it knows) is greater than that of either of its two neighbours (which it does not know) by sending this value to each of these neighbours, P_k and P_l say. These perform the necessary comparisons and if either k or l is found to be greater than i the corresponding process replaces P_i as candidate; otherwise P_i remains the candidate and tests this against a larger set of processes, in fact doubling the number of processes consulted. This continues until all the processes have been consulted. The subsequent role of a candidate defeated at any election is simply to pass any message received from one hand to the other, using **pass**.

The algorithm

Each process P_i carries the following declarations:

```
constant  my_number: value i;
variables state: position initialized not_involved;
          lgmax: integer;
          winner: integer;
          nbresp: 0, 1, or 2 initialized 0;
          respOK: boolean initialized T;
```

The type 'position' of the variable 'state' defines the possible states of a process in relation to the election in progress:

```
type position = (not_involved, candidate, lost, elected);
```

The messages relating to the election are of two types, declaring a candidature and responding to a candidature declaration respectively. Those of the first type are associated with the primitives **sendLR**, **pass** and have the form

(candidate, number, lg, lgmax)

where number is the identifier of the process sending the candidature message
      lg is the distance (length) around the ring already travelled by this message
      lgmax is the maximum distance the message must travel

The second type is associated with **pass** and **respond** and has the form

(response, bool, number);

where bool is T if the resonse is favourable ('respOK'), F otherwise
number is the identifier of the destination process (and is
therefore a means of addressing on the ring, since all the
identifiers are different)

The text for P_i is as follows.

```
when decision (initiate_election) do
                              state ← candidate;
                              lgmax ← 1;
                              while state = candidate do
                                    nbresp ← 0; respOK ← T;
                                      sendLR (candidature, my_number, 0,
                              lgmax);
                                    wait nbresp = 2;
                                    if respOK then state ← lost)
                                    end if;
                                    lgmax ← lgmax * 2;
                              end while;
                          end do;
when received (response, bool, number) do
                    if number = my_number then nbresp:= nbresp + 1;
                                    respOK:= respOK∧\bool;
                       else pass (response, bool, number);
                       end if;
                       end do;
when received (candidature, number, lgmax) do
                       case number < my_number then respond (response, F, number);
                       if state = not_involved then initiate_election;
                       end if;
                       end case;
                       case number > my_number then state ← lost;
                              lg ← lg + 1;
                              if lg < lgmax then pass (candidature, number, lg,
                              lmax);
                              else respond (response, T, number);
                              end if;
                              end case
                       case number = my_number then if state ≠ elected then state ←
                              elected;
                              winner ← my_number;
                              pass (ended, my_number);
                              end if;
                              end case;
                       end do;
when received (ended, number) do
                    if winner ≠ number then pass (ended, number);
                              winner ← number;
                              state ← not_involved;
                              end if;
                       end do;
```

Addressing
This is done implicitly in the algorithm. Taking a candidate process as origin, any other process is addressed by means of the length of the path from the origin to that process; and the destination of a response message, having a unique identifier, is recognized by the number carried by the message.

Number of messages
The length of the path travelled by any candidature message is of the form 2^i where i is some positive integer. A process P_j will launch its candidature on a path of length 2^i only if it has not been defeated in the election by a process whose distance from itself is at most 2^{i-1}:

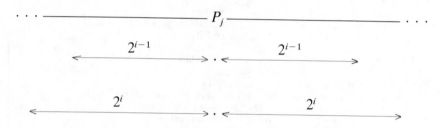

Further, in any set of $2^{i-1} + 1$ consecutive processes only one can launch a candidature on paths of length 2^i. Therefore, at the start of the procedure, although in the worst case all n processes can be candidates with paths of length 1, there are

at most $[n/2]$ that are candidates with paths of length 2
$\qquad$ $[n/3]$ that are candidates with paths of length 4
$\qquad$ $[n/(2^{i-1} + 1)]$ that are candidates with paths of length 2^i

Now a process that launches its candidature on a path of length 2^i will give rise to 2 messages (a candidature and a response) in each direction between each pair of processes on the path, at most; that is, to at most 4×2^i messages. So the total number of messages exchanged is at most

$$4 \times \left[1.n + 2\left(\frac{n}{2}\right) + 4\left(\frac{n}{3}\right) + \ldots + 2^i\left(\frac{n}{2^{i-1} + 1}\right) + \ldots \right]$$

Each term in this sum is the product of the number of paths and the length of those paths; none can exceed $2n$ in value and there are at most $(1 + \log n)$ terms, so an upper bound for the total number of messages is $8n(1 + \log n)$, which is $0(n \log n)$.

Thus this algorithm, although more complex than those mentioned at the end of Section 5.1, is more attractive because of the reduced number of messages.

5.4 The algorithm of Dolev, Klawe and Rodeh [DOL 82]

At the end of their paper (HIR 80] Hirschberg and Sinclair make the following conjecture: the number of messages needed by an elective algorithm on a *unidirectional* ring is $\Omega(n^2)$. If this were true it would imply that a bidirectional ring was needed to reduce the number of messages to a lower order. Many workers have sought either to prove or to disprove this conjecture and Dolev, Klawe and Rodeh disproved it by producing an algorithm needing $O(n \log n)$. We now describe this.

The principle of this algorithm – for a unidirectional ring, recall – consists in simulating a bidirectional algorithm as follows, in which we assume that the direction of flow of messages round the ring is from right to left for each process. A process P_i waits until it has received the identifiers of its two nearest neighbours on its right, say P_k, P_l where P_k is the nearer, that is between P_i and P_l. P_i then takes the point of view of P_k and looks to see if this process has the greatest identifier of the three; if so, P_i transmits this number and if not remains passive, from then on merely handing on messages that it receives. Thus initially there are n groups of three messages each; the first stage in the procedure consists of communication and comparison of identifiers as just described, at the end of which the number of active processes will have been divided by at least 2, for if P_i remains active its neighbour on the right necessarily becomes passive. Successive stages repeat this procedure, and at each stage the ring of active processes has to be respecified; the passive processes merely relay the messages. When stage m has been reached, a process that remains active in stage $m+1$ is necessarily one whose neighbour on the right has become passive at that stage.

The algorithm

To simplify the presentation

(a) we assume that all the processes decide to participate in the election; if that were not the case, a process would decide to participate on first receiving a message concerning the election;

(b) we shall not give the details of the means for disseminating the greatest identifier number when this has been found: a message of special type can transport this around the ring so that all processes are informed in a single turn.

Each process P_i carries the following declarations:

constant	my_number:	**value** i;
variables	state:	(active, passive) **initialized** passive;
	max:	**integer initialized** my_number;
	neighbourR:	**integer**;

The variable 'neighbourR' holds the identity of the first active processor on the right of P_i; 'max' holds the identity of the process whose point of view P_i has taken – recall that after obtaining the identifiers of its two nearest active neighbours P_i then behaves as the nearer one, which would have obtained the identifiers of its neighbours on the left and the right.

Messages of two types are needed to transmit the identifiers, so as to distinguish between the nearer and the further of the two active neighbours (the second being the right-hand neighbour of the first). These are of the form

$$(b, \text{number})$$

where b is either 1 or 2 according as 'number' is the identifier of the first or the second neighbour. As before, the primitive **sendL** is used to send a message to the neighbour on the left.

```
    when decision (initiate_election) do
                sendL (1, my_number);
                state ← active;
                end do;
    when received (1, number) do
                if state = active then
        if number ≠ max then sendL (2, number)
                        neighbourR ← number;
```

```
        else ⟨max is greatest number and is sent to all processes⟩;
          end if,
                          else sendL (1, number);
                          end if;
  end do;
  when recieved (2, number) do
                  if state = active then
                      if neighbourR > number and neighbourR > max then
                          max ← neighbourR;
                          sendL (1, neighbourR);
                      else state ← passive;
                      end if;
                  else sendL (2, number);
                  end if;
  end do;
```

As already stated, the role of a passive process is simply to pass to its neighbour on the left any message received from its neighbour on the right. Initially all the processes are active and each local variable max holds the number of its own process. Thus the first message received by each process is of the form (1, number), which enables it to update its variable neighbourR and to send the message (2, number) to its neighbour on the left. When a process P_i has received such a message it has three identifier numbers of active processes: max, giving its own number, neighbourR giving that of its first neighbour on the right and number giving that of the second. If neighbourR is the greatest of these, P_i takes over the role of that process by means of the instruction max ← neighbourR, remains active and sends the message (1, neighbourR) to start the next stage in the procedure; otherwise P_i becomes passive.

Types of message
Each active process receives messages of type (1, number) and (2, number) alternately, thus obtaining the identifiers of its first and second active neighbours on its right. Since the order is always (1, . . .) (2, . . .) (1,. . .) (2,. . .) . . . the identifier 1/2 is redundant and only the process identifier number need be sent; thus only n distinct messages are needed. However, we have preferred to follow [DOL 82] and distinguish between the two types, in the interests of clarity.

Validity of the algorithm; number of messages
We shall give only an indication of the principle of a formal proof

of the validity of the algorithm; detailed proofs are given in [DOL 82] and in [PET 82].

At any given stage in the calculation, after receiving the two numbers, the only processes that remain active are those P_i for which neighbourR is the maximum of the set of three, when $P_{\text{neighbourR}}$ becomes passive. P_i then takes over the role of $P_{\text{neighbourR}}$ and starts the next stage by performing **sendL** (1, neighbourR). Thus the maximum value that P_i has found remains in the election.

As we have seen, the number of processes remaining at this next stage is at most half the number of the stage just concluded; so if the procedure starts with n active processes, at most ($\log_2 n + 1$) stages are needed to reduce this number to 1, when the algorithm terminates, leaving a single process that knows the greatest identifier.

At each stage $2n$ messages are exchanged by the processes: there are n processes (active and passive together) and each issues one message of type (1, number) and one (2, number). At the final stage only one process is active so only n messages are exchanged. Thus the total is $2n \log n + n$, i.e. $O(n \log n)$.

5.5 Other algorithms

5.5.1 Franklin's algorithm [FRA 82]

This is an elective algorithm for a bidirectional ring. The principle is similar to that of [DOL 82] but advantage is taken of the bidirectional nature of the ring and an active process tests to see if its identifier is greater than those of its neighbours on both left and right; if it is not then the process becomes passive and, as before, simply relays any message recieved. Again, the number of processes left active is divided by at least 2 at each stage; and as $2n$ messages are exchanged at each stage the total number is $2n (1 + \log n)$, or $O(n \log n)$ again.

5.5.2 Peterson's algorithm [PET 82]

As we have seen, Hirschberg and Sinclair's conjecture (Section 5.4) was shown to be false by Dolev, Klawe and Rodeh by their demonstration of an $O(n \log n)$ algorithm; the same algorithm was given independently by Peterson, so Section 5.4 could equally well have been headed 'Peterson's algorithm'. Competition between these two groups of researchers has resulted in optimization of the algorithm: Dolev *et al.* reduced the number of messages to $1.5 \, n \log n + O(n)$, then Peterson to $1.44n \log n + O(n)$, then Dolev *et al.* to $1.33n \log n + O(n)$ . . . Burns has shown that the lower bound for the multiplier is 0.15, reached when n is a power of 2, and that this holds whether the ring is unidirectional or bidirectional.

5.5.3 The algorithm of Korach, Moran and Zaks [KOR 84]

These authors have investigated the upper and lower bounds for the numbers of messages required by various algorithms. They themselves have suggested an elective algorithm — 'the king and the subjects' in which all the processes are kings at the start and at the end there is only one king, all the others having become subjects. The algorithm is important on two counts: the topology of the interprocess connections is no longer a ring but a complete graph, and the number of messages is again $O(n \log n)$.

REFERENCES

[CAR 83]   CARVALHO, O., and ROUCAIROL, G., On Mutual Exclusion in Computer Networks, *Comm. ACM,* **26**(2) (Feb. 1983), pp. 146–147.

[CHA 79]   CHANGE, E. G., and ROBERTS, R., An Improved Algorithm for Decentralized Extrema-Finding in Circular Configurations of Processors, *Comm. ACM,* **22**(5) (May 1979), pp. 281–283.

[COR 81]   CORNAFION (group name), *Systèmes Informatiques Répartis*, Dunod (1981), 367 p.

[DIJ 65]   DIJKSTRA, E. W., Cooperating Sequential Processes. In F. Genuys (ed.) *Programming Languages*, Academic Press, New York (1965), pp. 43–112.

[DIJ 74]   DIJKSTRA, E. W., Self-Stabilizing Systems in Spite of Distributed Control, *Comm. ACM,* **17**(11) (Nov. 1974), pp. 643–644.

[DOL 82]   DOLEV, D., KLAWE, M., and RODEH, M., An $O(n \log n)$ Unidirectional Distributed Algorithm for Extrema Finding in a Circle, *Journal of Algorithms*, **3** (1982), pp. 245–260.

[FRA 82]   FRANKLIN, W. R., On an Improved Algorithm for Decentralized Extrema-Finding in Circular Configurations of Processors, *Comm. ACM,* **25**(5) (May 1982), pp. 336–337.

42

[HIR 80] HIRSCHBERG, D. S. and SINCLAIR, J. B., Decentralized Extrema Finding in Circular Configurations of Processors, *Comm. ACM*, **23**(11) (Nov. 1980), pp. 627–628.

[KOR 84] KORACH, E., MORAN, S., and ZAKS, S., Tight Lower and Upper Bounds for Some Distributed Algorithms for a Complete Networks of Processors, *TAP, ACM Conference* (1984), pp. 199–205.

[LAM 74] LAMPORT, L., A New Solution of Dijkstra's Concurrent Programming problem, *Comm. ACM*, **17** (8) (Aug. 1974), pp. 453–455.

[LAM 78] LAMPORT, L., Time, Clocks and the Ordering of Events in a Distributed System, *Comm. ACM*, **21**(7) (July 1978), pp. 558–565.

[LEL 77] LELANN, G., Distributed Systems: Towards a formal Approach, *IFIP Congress, Toronto* (Aug. **1977**), pp. 155–160.

[MIS 83] MISRA, J., Detecting Termination of Distributed Computations Using Markers, *Proc. of the 2nd ACM Conf. on Principles of Distributed Computing, Montreal* (Aug. **1983**), pp. 290–294.

[PET 82] PETERSON, G. L., An $O(n \log n)$ Unidirectional Algorithm for the Circular Extrema Problem, *ACM Toplas*, **4**(4), (Oct. 1982), pp. 758–762.

[PET 83] PETERSON, G. L., A New Solution to Lamport's Concurrent Programming Problem Using Small Shared Variables, *ACM, Toplas*, **5**(1) (Jan. 1983), pp. 56–65.

[PES 83] PETERSON, J. L., and SILBERSCHATZ, A., Operating Systmes Concepts, Addison Wesley (1983), 548 p.

[PLO 84] PLOUZEAU, N., and RAYNAL, M., Spécifier les Algorithmes Distribués en ADA: Uné approche Cirtique, *Actes des Journées AFCET-ADA, Paris*, **42** (Dec. 1984), pp. 148–62.

[RAY 86] RAYNAL, M., *Algorithms for Mutual Exclusion*, MIT Press (1986), 120 p.

[RIC 81] RICART G., and AGRAWALA, A. K., An Optimal Algorithm for Mutual Exclusion in Computer Networks, *Comm. ACM*, **24**(1)(Jan. 1981), pp. 9–17.

[RIC 83] RICART, G., and AGRAWALA, A. K., Author's response to 'On Mutual Exclusion in Computer Networks' by Carvalho and Roucairol, *Comm. ACM*, **26**(2) (Feb. 1983), pp. 147–148.

[SUZ 82] SUZUKI, I., and KASAMI, T., An Optimality Theory for Mutual Exclusion Algorithms in Computer Networks, *Proc. of the 3rd Int. Conf. on Distributed Computing Systems, Miami* (Oct. **1982**), pp. 365–370.

3

ALGORITHMS FOR DETECTION AND RESOLUTION OF DEADLOCK

1 INTRODUCTION

1.1 The problem of deadlock

Mutual blocking of processes, or deadlock, is a major problem in any system whose working depends on communication between processes that need access to common resources. It was first met in implementing operating systems and has generated a considerable body of literature, on both theoretical and practical aspects (e.g. [SHA 74], [CRO 75], [CHA 84]).

The term applies to the situation in which every member of a set of two or more processes is waiting for an event to occur that can only be made to occur by another member of the same set. For example, if each of three processes, $P1$, $P2$, $P3$ needs simultaneous and exclusive access to some two of a set of three resources $R1$, $R2$, $R3$, there is a deadlock when each process has seized one resource and is waiting for another process to release the second resource that it needs.

A graph-theoretical model can be used to formalize the problem, and so to define it precisely. The processes are represented by the nodes of a directed graph, and an arc from the node representing process P_i to that representing P_j shows that P_i is waiting for an event that must be brought about by P_j. Such a 'wait-for' graph will show the deadlocks at any instant; a detailed treatment is given in [RAY 86].

There is at present a renewed interest in algorithms for dealing with deadlocks. As we said, the problem first appeared in operating systems (for centralized machines), for which an excellent account is given in [SHA 74]. It has become important in connection with multi-user databases, each item being equivalent to a unique resource [GAR 83], [ULL 82]; and the introduction of distributed architectures, bringing the need for control of these, has led to the concept of a partitioned system that cannot be characterized by a global state [PES 83], [COR 81]. These new structures with their new problems have cast fresh light on the problem.

1.2 Characterization of deadlock situations

This can be based on the origin of the events that result in a deadlock: whether they arise in connection with allocation of resources or with communication of messages [CHA 83].

1.2.1 Deadlock in resource allocation

Consider a set of processes that communicate between themselves by means of messages and with a set of controllers (which are dedicated processes) that manage a set of resources. We are interested in the allocation of these resources, and for simplicity we shall assume that each resource is unique and can be accessed by only one process at a time – as in the case for a database.

A process P_i wishing to access a resource r sends a request to the controller in charge of this resource; if r is free it is allocated to P_i, otherwise P_i is halted, waiting for r to be released by the process P_j that is then using it. Thus P_i is *dependent* on P_j. More generally, a process P_i is said to be dependent on another process P_s if there is a chain of processes $P_i, P_j, \ldots .P_s$ in which each, with the exception of P_i. is using a resource for which its predecessor is waiting. The waiting processes are said to be passive.

A subset of the processes is in a deadlock situation when, with this generalized definition of dependence, one of its members is dependent on itself. The corresponding graph is then a cycle, all the processes are mutually dependent and so block each other; further, all the processes on a path leading to any node of the cycle are equally blocked.

In this model we have assumed that each resource is the only one of its kind and that access to it is exclusive. A graph-theoretical model can be constructed for the more general case in which these assumptions no longer hold, requiring a bipartite graph in which both processes and resources are represented by the nodes: the use of a resource R_y by a process P_j is indicated by a directed arc from R_y to P_j, whilst a directed arc from P_i to R_x shows that P_i is waiting for R_x. Many algorithms for the centralized case can be developed with the aid of this model, interesting accounts of which are given in [SHA 74] and [PES 83]. In a distributed system the resources are scattered over the various sites and access to them is regulated by control processes that have no knowledge of a global state of the system and must therefore make their decisions on the basis of local information: this necessitates different algorithms.

Formally, the conditions under which deadlock can result from resource allocation are as follows [PES 83]:

(a) No resource can be used by more than one process at a time (the exclusive access assumption).
(b) Certain resources are held by processes that are halted, waiting for other resources to become available.
(c) Resources can be freed only by the processes: nothing can override this.
(d) There is a cycle in the 'wait-for' graphs: this condition implies the three preceding.

It follows from these conditions that the aim of an algorithm that deals with deadlocks is either to prevent the formation of a cycle in the graph or to detect its actual or potential occurrence. The 'wait-for' graph can equally well be called the graph of conflicts [BER 81].

1.2.2 Resolution of resource-allocation deadlocks: principles

In accordance with the two approaches just stated, methods for solving the problem fall into two main classes, characterized by prevention of a cycle forming (a priori method) and detection of a cycle once formed (a posteriori method).

A priori method (prevention of a cycle forming)
Methods in this class are based on the principle that a cylce cannot be formed if each process requests and is granted, simultaneously, all the resources it needs. There are several ways of realizing this.

One method starts by imposing a strict order on the resources, and then requiring the processes to request resources in this order. Then if the resources are, in order, R_1, R_2, . . ., R_m, the resource R_i cannot be requested by process P_k, say, unless it has already obtained all the resources R_j that it needs, with all $j < i$. The fact that the ordering of the resources is strict prevents the formation of a cylce in the graph. There is, however, a major disadvantage to this (Havender's [HAV 68]) method, namely that as the processes have to request the resources in a specified order rather than in the order in which they need to be used, they monopolize the resources more than is necessary and consequently degrade the performance of the system as a whole.

A second method applies only if each process can state in advance its maximum needs for resources: given the set of statements from all the processes, the possibility or otherwise of a cycle being formed can be determined and an allocation is made only if it will not lead to a cycle at some stage. Such a method is used in the 'Banker' algorithm of Haberman [HAB 69], and a distributed version is given in [MAD 84].

It is important to note that, whether the system is centralized or distributed, these methods can be applied only when the resources needed by each process can be determined in advance. This is not always the case, for example for databases to which new items can be added dynamically. There is an interesting similarity between these methods and the two-phase protocol [ESW 76] for ensuring consistency of data: the 'a priori' principle is used in both.

A posteriori method (detection of a cycle when formed)
This consists in allowing the processes to request and obtain resources as they wish and then to examine the consequences of the formation of a cycle immediately or at some later stage. If a cycle is detected the conflict is resolved by choosing one of the constituent processes and requiring it to release resources appropriately. Criteria of efficiency and/or cost are used to make the choice of process, which then returns to the state it was in before making the request.

This method imposes no restrictions on the requests for resources and therefore can be used whether the resources are defined statically or dynamically.

Choice of method

These a priori and a posteriori methods could equally well be called pessimistic and optimistic methods respectively, especially in connection with databases where a granule specifies a resource. The reason for this is that the first takes the view that deadlocks are frequent and that it is therefore worth preventing them from occurring at the possible cost of some loss in performance resulting from resources being allocated unnecessarily far in advance of being needed, together with the extra cost of looking for a possible cycle before making an allocation; whilst the second believes they are rare and therefore allows allocations to be made without restraint, accepting the cost of detecting occasional cycles and of taking the necessary corrective action.

Thus the choice of method depends on a number of criteria, among which are the advance knowledge the processes have of the resources they will need, and the granularity in the case of a database: in this latter case the processes are called 'transactions', a transaction being an atomic event [ULL 82].

1.2.3 Distribution and pseudo-deadlock

We have emphasized that a distributed system is characterized by there being no global state of the system known to all the processes. The same applies to a distributed algorithm, in which each process knows only its own local state and has to base decisisons on this knowledge together with whatever information it receives from others. In such conditions it is important not to react to what are conveniently called pseudo-deadlocks.

The situation associated with this term can arise, for example, when there is a sequence of processes P_1, P_2, . . ., P_k such that P_i is halted waiting for a resource held by P_{i+1} and P_k is active. P_k issues first a message releasing the resource for which P_{k-1} is waiting and then a message requesting a resource held by P_1. If this second message reaches the cycle-detecting process before the first, this will register a deadlock; but this is a false, not a real deadlock, resulting from from there being no global state as there would be in a centralized system.

48

Thus a false or pseudo-deadlock is a deadlock that ceases to exist the moment it is detected, and should not be registered by a good detection algorithm for a distributed system. To ensure this it may be necessary to build some assumptions concerning the communication links into the algorithm.

1.2.4 Deadlock in message communication

Not only the mechanics of resource allocation can lead to a deadlock but also the communication of messages between the processes: a situation can arise in which each of a group of processes is waiting for a message from another member of the group, but there is no message in transit.

To consider this in more detail we use the formulation of [CHA 83]. With each passive process P_i — that is a process halted, waiting for a message — we associate what is called the *dependence set* DS of P_i, consisting of all the processes from which P_i is expecting a message: if the control structure is non-deterministic a process may be waiting for a message from more than one other process.

A deadlock in a set S of processes can be defined as follows:

(a) All the constituent processes of S are halted, waiting for messages.
(b) S contains the dependence set of every process included in S.
(c) No messages are in transit between any processes of S.

Any process P_i belonging to S is deadlocked because it can never receive a message that will release it.

As before, we can use a graphical representation with the processes as nodes and the fact that P_i is waiting for a message from P_k or P_1 or . . . shown by arcs directed from the P_i node to each of these nodes. A message from, say, P_k will release P_i, in effect delete all these arcs, so the presence of a cycle in the graph is not a sufficient condition for the detection of a deadlock. Consider the following example:

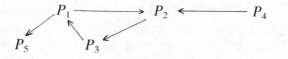

no deadlock

Here, P_1 is waiting for a message from either P_2 or P_5; P_5 is not waiting for any message and so can send a message to P_1 which thus becomes released and the arcs (P_1, P_2) and (P_1, P_5) deleted. For a deadlock, P_5 must be waiting for a message from one of the halted processes, i.e. $DS(P_5) \subseteq \{P_1, P_2, P_3, P_4\}$; this is illustrated below.

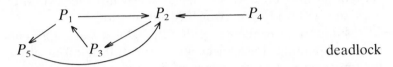

deadlock

In graph-theoretical terms the condition for deadlock in a set S of communicating processes is no longer the existence of a cycle, as it is in the resource-allocation case, but that all the successors of any member of S are themselves in S: that is, the S is a knot.

2 DISTRIBUTION OF A CENTRALIZED ALGORITHM: LOMET'S ALGORITHMS

2.1 Global and local states

One way of attacking the deadlock problem in a distributed context — that is when the processes and the resources are spread over a number of distinct sites — is to adapt a centralized algorithm to this context, and there are several ways in which this can be done. An obvious one is to specify a single allocator process for all the resources, to which all the processes of the system must send their requests for access to resources and their messages releasing resources. The allocator can base its actions on either the a priori or the a posteriori principle, thus either preventing a deadlock from occurring or detecting a potential deadlock and taking corrective action. As there is only one allocator process, its state at any instant can be taken as defining the global state of the system at that instant so far as resource allocation is concerned. The method has the great disadvantage that whilst it can be regarded as distributed from the point of view of mechanisms used — communication of messages — it is really only simulating a centralized procedure and therefore is exerting centralized control.

Another method involves replicating the means for averting or detecting deadlocks at every site, and this is the basis of Lomet's two algorithms [LOM 77, 79]. These, developed for database applications, use the a priori technique of preventing a deadlock from occurring. Their interest lies primarily in their methodology, the second optimizing the first: the first replicates the complete state of all the allocations on every site whilst the second provides each site with only a part of this information.

It is important to recognize that the 'global state' spoken of here is not something that can be known in full detail at any instant; it represents in fact the states of the resources as these are seen by the processes and of the relevant messages then in transit.

2.2 Lomet's first algorithm [LOM 77]: replication of the global state

As Lomet's algorithms were developed in the context of database work we shall speak of transactions rather than processes (cf. [COR 81]).

This first algorithm makes use of preliminary statements of need. A transactions T_j starts by stating the resources (here, blocks of data) that it will need. If some resource already being used by another transaction T_i forms part of T_j's need, a dependence relation (implying a potential conflict) between T_i and T_j is set up, shown on the corresponding graph G by a directed arc from T_j to T_i – that is, T_i potentially blocks T_j; and a potential deadlock is shown by a cycle in G. Thus the procedure is that a request is granted (i.e. a resource is allocated to the requesting transaction) only if the allocation will not create a cycle in the graph; otherwise the allocation is delayed until the resource over which there is conflict is released.

As an illustration, consider the classical example [COR 81, WAZ 83] of three transactions competing for three resources; these make the following statements:

transaction $T1$ $s11$ announces need for resources $R1$, $R2$
$s12$ requests $R1$
$s13$ requests $R2$
$T2$ $s21$ announces need for $R2$, $R3$
$s22$ requests $R2$

$s23$ requests $R3$

$T3$ $s31$ announces need for $R3$, $R1$

$s32$ requests $R3$

$s33$ requests $R1$

These actions are executed in the order $s11$, $s21$, $s31$, $s12$, $s13$, $s21$, $s22$, leading to the dependences $T2 \rightarrow T1 \rightarrow T3$.

Granting the request $s32$ (for $R3$) would block $T3$ because $R3$ forms part of $T2$'s stated needs and the allocation would create a cycle in the graph; so this is denied, even though at this stage $R3$ is not allocated.

Lomet distributes the algorithm by reproducing the graph — giving the state of the allocations — at each site, so that all the sites can make the same decision. The process of copying this global state to every site is managed in the same way as the copying of the queue in Lamport's mutual exclusion algorithm [LAM 78]: the statements of need, the requests and the messages releasing resources are sent to all the sites and are dealt with everywhere in the same order, so as to ensure consistency among the different copies; this single order is ensured by the use of time stamping.

2.3 Lomet's second algorithm [LOM 79]: use of partial state information

The algorithm just described is cumbersome to implement because every site has to know the entire global state in order to make its local decisions; the obvious question arises, could consistency still be guaranteed if each site managed its own resources on the basis of a knowledge of only part of this global state? — that is, of some subgraph of G?

Suppose each site keeps a graph of potential conflicts that concerns only those transactions whose needs include resources managed by that site; such a local graph will be a 'projection' of the full graph G on to that site. Taking the previous example again, suppose the resources $R1$, $R2$, $R3$ are managed by the sites $C1$, $C2$, $C3$ respectively; then the sequence of actions

$s11$, $s21$, $s31$, $s12$, $s22$, $s32$

52

will lead to the following local states:

at $C1$, managing $R1$	$T1 \rightarrow T3$
at $C2$, managing $R2$	$T2 \rightarrow T1$
at $C3$, managing $R3$	$T3 \rightarrow T2$

from which it will be seen that knowledge of these local states will not suffice, for none of the local graphs has a cycle although there is one in the global graph, and therefore no site will detect the potential conflict.

Lomet's solution consists in replacing the original condition for allowing a resource to be allocated — that this must not create a cycle in the graph G — by a stronger condition that can be verified locally [AND 83]. First, a strict ordering of the transactions is established: this can be based, for example, on time-stamping, each transaction carrying throughout its lifetime the time-stamp of its creation. These stamps being all different, a strict order can then be defined by saying that T_i precedes T_j if and only if the time-stamp of T_i is less than that of T_j. The local graph is now constructed to show both the potential dependences concerning the local resources, and the order relations among the transactions. It can be shown (cf. [COR 81]) that for there to be a cycle in the global graph G there must be a cycle in at least one of these local graphs; so a request for a resource at a particular site will not be granted if the allocation would produce a cycle in the corresponding local graph.

Taking the previous example once again, with the order $T1 \rightarrow T2 \rightarrow T3$ of the transactions, the graphs after the sequence of actions

$s11, s21, s31, s12$

would give

at $C1$, managing $R1$	$T1 \rightarrow T3$
at $C2$, managing $R2$	$T1 \rightarrow T2$
at $C3$, managing $R3$	$T2 \rightarrow T3$

Execution of $s22$ ($T2$ requesting $R2$) would block $T2$ because this allocation would create a cycle in the graph at $C2$: $T1$ has included $R2$ in its statement of needs and is given priority because it was created before *T*2; so the request is not granted. All this, of course, requires that the preliminary statements of needs and the time-stamps of the transactions are broadcast to all the sites.

It will be seen from this example that the use of partial states that are consistent with the global state (which latter is an abstraction, never actually represented) reduces the number of messages needed by the algorithm. However, the advantage is bought at the cost of a possible reduction in performance, as in this case where *T*2 is halted waiting for *R*2.

[COR 81] comments that this algorithm is based on a principle analogous to that of Havender's 'ordered resources' [HAV 68]. But in the present case the order is imposed not on the resources but on the transactions and this removes the risk of starvation, because a transaction will in effect become older, and therefore acquire higher priority, at the sites to which it has sent its requests as its predecessors complete their execution.

The advantages of this algorithm are that the distributed handling of deadlocks preserves the autonomy of the separate sites and the use of the a priori method prevents a transaction from being cancelled. But it cannot be applied if the resources can be varied dynamically, for then the system of advance statement of needs is no longer practical.

3 THE ROSENKRANTZ, STEARNS AND LEWIS ALGORITHM [ROS 78]

3.1 Principle of the algorithm: use of time-stamping

As we have just seen, Lomet's algorithms for warning of potential deadlocks are based on the idea of distributing a centralized algorithm, with an ordering defined by time-stamping introduced so as to control this distribution in a manner proper to a distributed algorithm. In his first algorithm a knowledge of the stamps (logical time + site number) of all the messages enables all sites to have the same view of the graph of potential conflicts and so to take consistent decisions. In his second the ordering is imposed on the transactions which are then required to take account of the order at each site.

54

The question now arises, could an algorithm for detection of deadlocks be based solely on time-stamps? Rosenkrantz, Stearns and Lewis have produced such an algorithm; like Lomet's it concerns database transactions, the consistency of the data being assumed to be ensured by systematic use of the two-phase protocol of Eswaran *et al.* [ESW 76].

If a resource R already being used ('locked up') by a transaction $T1$ is requested by another transaction $T2$ the conflict is resolved by comparison of their time-stamps. No advance statements of needs are made by the transactions, so the algorithm for this procedure is applicable when the access to the resources can vary dynamically. The purpose of the algorithm is to warn of potential deadlocks, comparison of the time-stamps then being used to prevent the cycle forming in the graph; the difference from Lomet's algorithms is that the procedure is now dynamic, so that one can speak of continuous avoidance of deadlock.

Two methods have been suggested in connection with this algorithm, called by the authors 'wait–die' and 'wound–wait' respectively.

3.2 'Wait–die' method

Suppose there are two transactions $T1$, $T2$ and a resource R that is being used by $T2$ and is requested by $T2$; let the time-stamps of the transactions, according to which they are put in strict order, be $e(T1)$, $e(T2)$. The allocator at the site of R then acts according to the following algorithm:

```
if e(T2) < e(T1) then halt T2 ('wait')
              else kill T2 ('die')
end if
```

This means that if $T2$ is the older it remains halted until $T1$ releases R, either by terminating normally or by being 'killed' when requesting another resource; if it is the younger, $T2$ is removed from the contest and must return later, with the same time-stamp as before.

Thus the time-stamps define an order of priority among the transactions and the one of highest priority is never killed; further, since a killed transaction is revived later with its original time stamp it grows older and therefore gains increased priority and so, even if killed several times, is never removed completely from the contest.

No site needs to know the state of allocation of all the resources; the only items of information needed are the time-stamps of the transactions that request its own resources, and these are fixed once and for all, independently of the separate sites.

3.3 'Wound–wait' method

In the wait-die algorithm a transaction $T2$ that requests access to a resource R that is being used by another transaction $T1$ is killed if $T2$ is the younger or halted until R is released if $T1$ is the younger. An alternative strategy is to grant all the requests of the highest priority (i.e. the oldest) transaction at any stage by killing all the younger transactions that are using the required resources: this is the wound–wait method.

With, as before, $T2$ requesting resource R that is being used by $T1$ the algorithm for the site of R is as follows:

```
if e(T2) < e(T1) then kill T1 ('wound')
              else halt T2 ('wait')
end if
```

In contrast to 'wait–die', a transaction never has to wait for a resource being used by a younger transaction.

3.4 Comments on these algorithms

The two algorithms just described have the advantage of simplicity: the time-stamping determines the relative priorities when any conflict arises, and since this ordering is the same for all sites the decisions taken by the local allocators are consistent. They apply, however, only to the resolution of conflicts concerning resource allocation; they were developed in the context of access to distributed databases, in which no conflict arises if the various transactions are accessing disjoint sets of data.

The allocation algorithms take into account only the requester and the current user of the resource that is the cause of the conflict; for completeness they should consider also any other transactions that could be halted and waiting for that resource. Wazdi [WAZ 83] has studied the case in which at most one other transaction is thus halted (all others having been killed) and also that where there is no limit to this number. For this first case he has shown that if $T3$ requests a resource for which $T2$ is waiting while it is being used by $T1$, the first necessity is to use the wound–wait algorithm to resolve the conflict between $T2$ and $T3$, and then to use either algorithm to resolve the remaining conflict for the resource. In the second the halted transactions must be queued in order of increasing time-stamp number (i.e. decreasing age) and the wound–wait algorithm used (only this will ensure freedom from starvation): the time-stamp of the newly requesting transaction is compared with those of the halted transactions and only if this is the oldest transaction is its request considered, again using wound–wait.

Finally, it must be noted that if a conflict is resolved by any method that involves killing transactions, whilst this is effective it can kill transactions that would not have led to any deadlock; and these premature killings can start a chain reaction that may reduce the performance of the system as a whole. The effect is particularly significant with the wait–die strategy. Balter *et al.* [BAL 82] have investigated these problems by simulation and have concluded that deadlock-detecting algorithms must not be allowed to create bottlenecks in a distributed system; the algorithms just described are valuable when there are only few conflicts.

4 ALGORITHMS FOR DETECTING DEADLOCKS

4.1 Proposed methods

The basic principle for detecting a deadlock produced by resource allocation is the same whether the system is centralized or distributed: examine the graph for cycles. A global view of this graph is not possible when the resources are distributed over a number of sites, so any algorithm must take into account the fact that the graph also is distributed over the different sites.

Each site must now keep up-to-date that part of the graph that refers to its own resources — the local graph. A cycle here indicates a local deadlock, but the problem is to detect cycles in the global graph. Several approaches are possible, depending on whether the system control is centralized, hierarchical or distributed.

4.2 Algorithms with centralized control

In such algorithms one particular site is given the task of keeping up to date the graph of conflicts and detecting deadlocks (cf. Section 2.1); all the other sites inform this site of their requests for, and releasing of, resources. This is a simple solution of the problem but has several disadvantages: failure of the monitoring site is fatal, the number of messages needed is large and no use is made of the autonomy of the separate sites — that is, a potential cycle at a single site is not detected locally. There is also the risk of signalling pseudo-deadlocks, depending on the speeds with which different messages are transmitted (cf. Section 1.2.3). Stonebraker's algorithms [STO 79], used in the Ingres distributed database system, and that of Gray [GRA 78] are of this type.

4.3 Algorithms with hierarchical control

In this case the separate sites maintain graphs for local conflicts, that is, conflicts concerning only the processes that are either using or waiting for the resources they manage. The complete set of sites is organized as a tree structure in which each node, apart from the leaf (terminal) nodes, generates a graph that contains all the information needed for the complete set of corresponding graphs generated by its descendants. Thus a deadlock that involves a group of transactions is detected by the site represented in the tree as the common ancestor of all the sites whose resources are among the objects of the conflict. This hierarchical scheme was suggested by Menasce and Muntz [MEN 79].

4.4 Algorithms with distributed control

Distributing control in the detection of deadlocks means abolishing all forms of hierarchy among the sites; each separate site then retains its autonomy and a local failure is not fatal to the algorithm as a whole. A rather naïve way of achieving this is to use the same principle as is used in Lomet's first algorithm: a copy of the graph of halted processes is maintained at every site, with the result that every site has a global view of the system. This is done in the algorithm of Isloor and Marsland [ISL 78].

The algorithms of Gligor and Shattuck [GLI 80] and of Obermark [OBE 82] detect cycles without needing this global knowledge; Obermark's is used in the distributed database system R* developed by IBM [LIN 84]. Ho and Ramamoorthy [HOR 82] give a set of protocols for detecting deadlocks, suitable for database work.

5 DEADLOCKS DUE TO COMMUNICATIONS: ALGORITHM OF CHANDY, MISRA AND HAAS [CHA 83]

5.1 Resumé: features of the problem

We touched on this problem in Section 1.2.4 where we introduced the concept of the *dependence set* (DS) of a process: $DS(P_i)$ denotes the set of all processes from which P_i is waiting for a message at the instant considered, a non-deterministic form of control being assumed. If P_i is active at this instant then $DS(P_i)$ is empty; and as P_i may expect messages from different sources its dependence set, when not empty, may vary with time as the algorithm is executed.

What characterizes a deadlock in a set S of processes is that every process P_i belonging to S is halted and every member of $DS(P_i)$ is a member of S; and no messages are being transmitted between members of S. In graph-theoretical terms, detecting such a situation reduces to detecting a knot in the graph of waiting processes; this is the objective of the algorithm of Chandry, Misra and Haas [CMH].

5.2 Assumptions and principles underlying the algorithm

This is a distributed algorithm, meaning that there is no co-ordinating process; it is assumed that the transmission time of a message is arbitrary but finite, so that there is no loss of messages, and that messages are received in the order in which they were sent. Further, the topology of the communication system is identical with that of the program formed by the processes, so that there is no need for a special system for message communication in addition to that provided to link the processes.

The CMH algorithm is based on the 'diffusing computation' principle (cf. Chapter 1, Section 4.2.1): a passive process (i.e. a process halted and waiting for a message concerning the text of the program it is executing) launching a diffusing computation to determine whether or not it is deadlocked, in which only passive processes can participate; several processes may launch such a procedure and a single process may launch several.

A launching process is called an initiator. For any initiator P_i the structure of the computation that it launches is as follows: represented as a tree, P_i is the root, the members of $DS(P_i)$ are its descendants, and so on. The criterion for deadlock detection is that if the computation initiated by P_i ends normally (i.e. if all the expected replies are received) then P_i is deadlocked.

5.3 The CMH algorithm

Messages and their use
Messages of two types are used in this procedure, *question* and *answer*. The first searches the initiator's graph to identify the processes in the dependence set of this process, then the dependence sets of its descendants and so on; the second reports the results of this search to be the initiator. The form of either message is

(question/answer i,m,j,k)

in which the origin and destination of the message are defined by j, k respectively, whilst the pair (i,m) defines uniquely the diffusing computation to which the message is reported: i is the initiator and m its position in the order of the detection operations launched by i. The meanings of these indices are explained more fully in the following paragraphs.

The way in which the messages are used in the computation is as follows. When a process P_j is made aware that a new detection operation is in progress, by receiving the message

(question i,m,l,j)

from P_l it sends messages

(question $i,m,\ j,k$)

to every member P_k of its dependence set $DS(P_j)$, and replies to P_l with the message

(answer $i\ m,\ j,l$)

when it has received all the answer messages in reply to its questions. P_j acts in this way only if it is inactive when it receives P_l's question and remains so between sending out its questions and receiving any replies. 'Inactive' here means that it is not performing its own processing; from the point of view of the diffusing computation it is active.

Variables

Each process P_i uses certain local variables so as to record its own view of the global state. There are five of these, taking the form of arrays indexed by the numbering of the set of processes, together with a constant that identifies the particular process:

constant   my_number **value** i
variables last: **array** $[1, \ldots, n]$ **of integer initialized** 0
         number: **array** $[1, \ldots, n]$ **of integer**
         wait: **array** $[1, \ldots, n]$ **of boolean initialized** F
         parent: **array** $[1, \ldots, n]$ **of** $1, \ldots, n$
         state: (active, passive)

The meanings of these are:

> *last* contains the order numbers of the last deadlock detection operations launched by the processes constituting the system,

with which P_i has been concerned. Thus last $[j]$ contains the largest value of m received by P_i in a message (question j, last $[j]$, i, k)

number $[j]$ gives the number of messages of the form (question j,last$[j]$,i,k) sent out by P_i that have not been acknowledged by a response from a member P_k of DS(P_i) with a message of the form (answer j, last$[j]$, k, i)

wait $[j]$ is a boolean, T if P_i has remained inactive since the passage of the first message (question j, last$[j]$, *, i) ('inactive' meaning as before)

parent $[j]$ contains the number of the process that has sent to P_i the first detection message (j, last$[j]$); parent$[j]$ is the number of the process that is P_i's parent in the diffusing computation that concerns this detection.

In addition to these variables concerned with the deadlock detection there has to be something to define the dependence set of P_i at any instant; this is provided by a variable dep_set declared with P_i:

> variable   dep_set: **set of** 1, . . ., n

This is up-dated by the process P_i itself whenever it sets itself to wait for a message. It is used by the deadlock detection algorithm, where it provides the interface between the controlled process and the controller.

Behaviour at a site

As already explained, when a process P_i receives a question message it broadcasts this to all members of its dependence set as constituted in that instant. Possible cycles in the graph of dependence can be detected with the aid of the variable last, as follows. Suppose P_i receives the message (question j, m, k, i); if m is strictly greater than last$[j]$ this is the first message concerning the detection identified by (j, m). The variable last$[j]$ is therefore up-dated with the received value m and the question message broadcast to all the processes in dep_set. If m is equal to last$[j]$ the message is returned to P_i; there is thus a cycle in the graph of dependences and P_i does not broadcast the message but replies by sending (answer j, m, i, k). Finally, if m is less than last$[j]$ the message is ignored: P_i takes account only of messages received while it remains halted waiting for responses to the corresponding question.

The program text for P_i is as follows.

```
when decision launch detection and state = passive do
      last(i) ← last(i) + 1; wait(i) ← T;
            for j∈dep_set do send (question i, last(i), i, j) to j;
            end for;
            number(i) ← cardinal(dep_set);
      end do;
received message different from question/answer do
      state ← active; wait(i) ← F ∨ i;
      end do;
received (question k, m, j, i) and state = passive do
if m > last(k) then begin
            last (k) ← m;
            parent(k) ← j;
            wait(k) ← T;
            for r ∈ dep_set do send (question k, m, i, r) to r;
                        end do;
            end for;
            number(k) ← cardinal(dep_set);
            end;
            else if wait(k) and m = last(k) then send (answer k,m,i,j) to j;
            end if;
      end if;
      end do;
received (answer k, m, r, i) and state = passive do
      if m = last(k) and wait(k) then begin
      number(k) ← number(k) − 1;
      if number(k) = 0 then if k = i then P_i deadlocked; else send
                        (answer k,m,i,parent(k)) to parent(i);
                                    end if;
                  end if;
                  end;
      end if;
      end do;
```

Comments on the algorithm

(a) An active process – that is, a process that is not waiting for messages – rejects any question/answer messages addressed to it; the effect is that its questioners, not receiving the answers they expected, cannot declare themselves to be deadlocked.

(b) As can be seen from the program text for P_i the variables number(k) and parent(k) form the manifestation of the graph for the diffusing computation initated by P_k. There can be at most n such trees, reached if every one of the n processes is inactive and initiates a deadlock detection.

(c) The algorithm deals only with processes that are passive and waiting for messages, i.e. such that dep_set $\neq 0$. It can be modified to deal with terminated processes, meaning processes that are passive but are not waiting for any message, and whose dependence set is therefore empty; when such a process receives a question message it always responds with an answer. To distinguish between deadlocked and terminated processes it is sufficient to examine the dependence set: if this is empty the process is terminated, if not it is deadlocked; it also serves to detect complete blocking of processes waiting for messages from processes that have terminated. The figure below shows how a knowledge of the termination of P_i is important for the detection of deadlocking of the other processes.

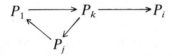

(d) [CHA 83] shows that the algorithm has the following properties, which we only list here:
   (i) If the initiator of a detection computation is deadlocked at the time, it will be detected as deadlocked.
   (ii) If a process declares itself deadlocked, it is a member of a set of deadlocked processes.
   (iii) If each process initiates a detection computation every time it becomes passive, at least one process in each deadlocked set will be detected as deadlocked.
   The assumption that messages between any pair of processes are received in the order in which they were sent is used in establishing these properties; it provides a guarantee of the consistency of information.
   A fourth, important, property follows from the above:
   (iv) The algorithm does not report pseudo-deadlocks.

(e) The algorithm does not detect the absence of deadlock. If a process P_i initiates a detection computation there are only two possible events that can occur: either the diffusing computation ends with P_i declaring itself deadlocked, or P_i receives a message that reactivates it. The event recording that P_i is not a member of a deadlocked set occurs, but this does not indicate that the other processes are not deadlocked.

(f) An important feature of the algorithm is that, because it is executed only by halted processes, it does not lead to any loss in performance. In the diffusing computation each process sends a message to every member of its dependence set and gets at most one response from each; so if the total number of members of all the dependence sets taken together is k this gives a maximum of $2nk$ messages. In the extreme case of a fully connected topology, with every process waiting for a message from every other, the number is $2n(n-1)$.

Another important parameter is the length of the time interval after which a passive process relaunches a deadlock detection; this must be chosen appropriately if the algorithm is to work well (cf. [GRA 78]).

5.4 Other algorithms

The CMA algorithm, modified to take account of terminated processes (i.e. processes whose dependence sets are empty) can be applied to detect the termination of a set E of processes. This is achieved by adding a special process P_s whose dependence set is E itself: if P_s declares itself deadlocked then every process P_e of E is also deadlocked and therefore terminated. The nature of this termination is evaluated with the help of the variables dep_set: if dep_set(P_e) is empty then P_e has terminated normally, so if this holds for every member of E then the complete set E has terminated normally.

It will be seen from this that deadlock and termination are related problems [MIS 82]; there are even algorithms for which deadlock is the 'normal' termination [FRA 80]. We shall consider the question of termination in the next chapter.

The CMA algorithm can be adapted also to detect knots; and finally, it has been adapted to deal with the case in which communications are defined, not by processes, but by names of ports [NAT 84].

REFERENCES

[AND 83]   ANDRE, F., HERMAN, D., and VERJUS, J. P., *Synchronisation des Programmes Parallèles*, Dunod (1983), 138 p. [English translation, S. J. Howlett: *Synchronization of Parallel*

Programs, North Oxford Academic (Kogan Page) (1985), 108 p.]

[BAL 82]   BALTER, R., BERARD, P., and DECITRE, P., Why Concurrency level in Distributed Systems is more Fundamental than Deadlock management, *Proc. of ACM-SIGART-SIGOPS Symp. on Principles of Distributed Computing, Ottawa* (Aug. **1982**).

[BER 81]   BERNSTEIN, P. A., and GOODMAN, N., Concurrency Control in Distributed Data Base Systems, *Computing Surveys*, **13**(2) (June 1981), pp. 185–221.

[CHA 83]   CHANDY, K. M., MISRA, J., and HAAS, L. M., Distributed Deadlock Detection, *ACM TOCS*, **1**(2) (May 1983), pp. 144–156.

[CHA 84]   CHANDY, K. M., and MISRA, J., The Drinking Philosophers Problem, *ACM Toplas*, **6**(4) (Oct. 1984), pp. 632–696.

[COR 81]   CORNAFION (group name), *Systèmes Informatiques Répartis*, Dunod (1981), 368 p.

[CRO 75]   CROCUS (group name), *Systèmes d'Exploitation des Ordinateurs*, Dunod (1975), 364 p.

[DIJ 80]   DIJKSTRA, E. W., and SCHOLTEN, C. S., Termination Detection for Diffusing Computations, *Inf. Processing Letters*, **11**(1) (Aug. 1980), pp. 1–4.

[ESW 76]   ESWARAN, K. P., GRAY, J. N., LORIE, R. A., and TRAIGER, I. L., The Notions of Consistency and Predicate Locks in a Data Base System, *Comm. ACM*, **18**(11) (Nov. 1976), pp. 624–633.

[FRA 80]   FRANCEZ, N., Distributed Termination, *ACM Toplas*, **2**(1) (Jan. 1980), pp. 42–55.

[GAR 83]   GARDARIN, G., Bases de Données: les Systèmes et leurs landages, Eyrolles (1983), 266 p.

[GLI 80]   GLIGOR, D., and SHATTUCK, S. H., On Deadlock Detection in Distributed Systems, *IEEE Trans. on SE*, **6**(5) (Sept. 1980), pp. 435–440.

[GRA 78]   GRAY, J. N., Notes on Data Base Operating Systems, *LNCS* **60**, Springer Verlag (1978), pp. 393–481.

[HAB 69]   HABERMAN, A. N., Prevention of Systems Deadlock, *Comm. ACM*, **12**(7) (July 1969), pp. 373–377.

[HAV 68]   HAVENDER, J. W., Avoiding Deadlocks in Multitasking Systems, *IBM System Journal*, **7**(2) (1968), pp. 74–84.

[HOL 71]   HOLT, R. C., Comments on Prevention of Systems Deadlock, *Comm. ACM*, **14**(1) (Jan. 1971), pp. 36–38.

[HOR 82]   HO, G. S., and RAMAMOORTHY, C. V., Protocols for Deadlock Detection in Distributed Data Base Systems, *IEEE Trans. on SE*, **8**(6) (Nov. 1982), pp. 554–557.

[ISL 78]   Isloor, S. S., and Marsland, T. A., The Deadlock Problem: an Overview, *Computer,* **13**(9) (Sept. 1980), pp. 58–78.

[LAM 78]   Lamport, L., Time, Clocks and the Ordering of Events in a Distributed System, *Comm. ACM,* **21**(7) (July 1978), pp. 558–565.

[LIN 84]   Lindsay, B. G. *et al.*, Computation and Communication in R*: a Distributed Database Manager, *ACM TOCS,* **2**(1) (Feb. 1984), pp. 24–38.

[LOM 77]   Lomet, D. B., A practical Deadlock Avoidance Algorithm for Data Base Systems, *Proc. ACM-SIGMOD Conf. on Management of Data* (**1977**), pp. 122–127.

[LOM 79]   Lomet, D. B., *Coping with Deadlock in Distributed Systems,* Data Base Architecture, North Holland (1979), pp. 95–105.

[MAD 84]   Madduri, H., and Finkel, R., Extension of the Banker Algorithm for Resource Allocation in a Distributed Operating System, *Inf. Processing Letters,* **19**(1) (1984), pp. 1–8.

[MEN 79]   Menasce, D. A., and Muntz, R. R., Locking and Deadlock Detection in Distributed Data Base, *IEEE Trans. on SE,* **5**(3) (May 1979), pp. 195–202.

[MIS 82]   Misra, J., and Chandy, K. M., Termination Detection of Diffusing Computations in CSP, *ACM Toplas,* **4**(1) (Jan. 1982),. pp. 37–43.

[NAT 84]   Natarajan, N., A Distributed Algorithm for Detecting Communication Deadlock, *LNCS,* **181**, Springer Verlag (1984), pp. 119–135.

[OBE 82]   Obermarck, R., Distributed Deadlock Detection Algorithm, *ACM TODS,* **7**(2) (June 1982), pp. 187–208.

[PES 93]   Peterson, J. L., and Silberschatz, A., *Operating Systems Concepts,* Addison-Wesley (1983), 548 p.

[RAY 86]   Raynal, M., *Algorithms for Mutual Exclusion,* MIT Press, (1986), 120 p.

[ROS 78]   Rosenkrantz, D. J., Stearns, R. E., and Lewis, P. M., System Level Concurrency Control in Distributed Data Base, *ACM TODS,* **3**(2) (June 1978), pp. 178–198.

[SHA 74]   Shaw, A. C., The Logical Design of Operating Systems, Prentice-Hall (1974), 306 p.

[STO 79]   Stonebraker, M., Concurrency Control and Consistency of Multiplie Copies of Data in Distributed INGRES, *IEEE Trans. on SE,* **5**(3) (May 1979).

[ULL 82]   Ullmann, J. D., *Principles of Data Base Systems* (2nd edn), Computer Science Press (1982), 484 p.

[WAZ 83]   Wazdi, F., *Etude de l'Interblocage dans les Systèmes Répartis,* Thèse Docteur Ingénieur, Université de Montpellier (1983).

4

ALGORITHMS FOR DETECTING TERMINATION

1 INTRODUCTION: THE PROBLEM OF TERMINATION

1.1 Distributed termination

The problem of detecting that a distributed algorithm has terminated is both important and non-trivial. Even if observation has shown that all the constituent processes of the algorithm are in a passive state — that is, are not active — this cannot be taken as proof that the algorithm as a whole has terminated: for a process observed to be passive may be reactivated by a message from a process that has not yet been observed and which then becomes passive. The problem would be simple if knowledge were available, at any instant, of a global state that took into account both the processes and the communication channels. Designing an algorithm for the problem thus comes down to designing a distributed control mechanism that will recognize a particular state of global stability, that of termination.

We must first define some terms. A process is said to be active if it is executing the text of its program and passive if it is in any other state. A passive process can be either terminated, having completed its task, or waiting for messages from other processes. If all the processes are passive and no messages are in transit the complete distributed algorithm is said to be terminated. We can assign a 'quality' to the terminated state and set up a means for determining this: with each process P_i is associated a local predicate B_i which when P_i is passive takes the value T if P has terminated normally and F otherwise. When the termination of the complete algorithm is detected, an examination of the set of predicates B_i will show whether the calculation represented by the algorithm has or has not been completed satisfactorily [FRR 82].

1.2 Termination and deadlock

Suppose that in executing a certain case a distributed algorithm consisting of a set of processes has reached a state in which every process is waiting for a message from another. One way to detect the termination in such a case would be to show that the entire set of processes is deadlocked and therefore cannot become active again; and in such a case deadlock and termination present the same problem. Thus it is natural to ask what is the relation between the two in general, and what do these two states have in common.

So far as deadlock is concerned, we saw in the previous chapter that two attitudes to this are possible, one of warning of a potential deadlock and the other of detection of an actual deadlock. For termination, where the problem is to decide whether or not an algorithm has completed the calculation intended, the only possible attitude is that of detection — warning of impending termination does not make sense: however, it is quite another problem to prove that the algorithm *will* always terminate.

Detecting a deadlock in a set S of processes constituting a distributed algorithm reduces to detecting such a situation in a subset T of S; the remaining processes (the set $S - T$), not being deadlocked, will be either active or terminated. Here the subset T is not defined in advance but becomes defined dynamically, whilst in the termination problem the situation is entirely different and we are interested in establishing the termination of all the processes of S, not of some subset determined a posteriori. If we were interested in the termination of some subset of S, that subset would be determined in advance. Thus there is a fundamental difference: in the case of termination we are seeking to show that a given set of processes possesses a certain property whilst in the case of deadlock we are looking for a set of processes that possesses a certain (different) property.

A further difference between deadlock and termination concerns the way in which the processes become passive. In a deadlocked set all the processes are halted and waiting for messages; in termination the passive processes are either waiting for messages or have completed their tasks.

Thus deadlock and termination are related but distinct problems, and it is important not to confuse them.

1.3 Principles underlying the solutions

As we have just said, detecting termination is a matter of showing that a given set of processes has a given property — that of termination. By the nature of the problem the set is defined in advanced (in what follows we shall assume that it contains all the processes) and all the methods proposed for attacking the problem start by imposing a structure on this set so that it can be scanned in order to check that the property holds. The basic structures that have been proposed are the unidirectional ring [DIJ 83, RAN 83], a spanning tree for the graph of the processes [DIJ 80, FRR 82, TOP 84] and a predefined cycle in this graph [MIS 83, RAN 83] — this last differs from the ring structure in that the same process can occur several times in the cycle.

The structure having been settled, the next requirement is to settle the method of scanning so that pseudo-terminations are not recorded, that is, a situation in which a process that has been observed to be passive is reactivated by a message sent from another process which then itself becomes passive; if the chosen structure is a spanning tree this can be achieved by means of a diffusing computation, if a ring or a cycle by means of a circulating token (cf. Chapter 1).

We now describe four algorithms for this detection, based on four different techniques: diffusing computation, 'coloured' tokens, cycle of processes and time-stamping respectively.

2 USE OF DIFFUSING COMPUTATION: ALGORITHM OF DIJKSTRA AND SCHOLTEN [DIJ 80]

2.1 Assumptions

The idea of the diffusing computation, due to Dijkstra and Scholten, was discussed briefly in Chapter 1; it is a particular method of communication between processes. The communication channels between the processes enable a directed graph to be defined, of which the processes form the nodes; a special node (i.e. process) is defined that has no parent and therefore cannot receive any messages, called the *environment*. Initially all the processes are passive and the diffusing computation starts with the environment sending one or more messages to one or more of its descendants.

A process becomes active only after receiving its first message, when it in turn can send messages to its descendants in the graph. The assumptions are made that a process can send only a finite number of messages and that the transmission times of the messages, though arbitrary, are finite.

With this framework Dijkstra and Scholten state the problem as follows: how to adapt the diffusing computation to give a check for termination such that the environment process is informed when the computation is completed but is not informed of any pseudo-termination.

2.2 Basis of the algorithm

All the processes being passive initially, except the environment which sends messages to descendants in the graph G, the basic idea is to associate with each message sent by a process P_i to another process P_j a special message, or 'signal', from P_j to P_i; these signals form a special kind of acknowledgement and their issuing is subject to a rule that expresses the property of termination in such a way that when the environment process has received acknowledgements of all the messages it has issued, it concludes that the diffusing computation is completed.

To achieve this the concept of *deficit* is introduced, concerning the communication between pairs of processes: this is a number associated with each unidirectional communication channel between a pair of processes (i.e. with each directed arc of the graph G) and is the difference between the number of messages received and the number of signals sent over that channel. Two non-negative integers, defin and defout, defined for each process P_i, respectively count the sums of the deficits of the arcs entering the corresponding node and those leaving it, both set to 0 initially. These counters can be used to formulate a rule that will govern the issuing of messages and acknowledgement signals in such a way as to guarantee that termination is detected.

For each process, defin and defout are manipulated as follows:

message issued	defout	$\leftarrow$ defout $+ 1$
signal issued	defin	$\leftarrow$ defin $- 1$
message received	defin	$\leftarrow$ defin $+ 1$
signal received	defout	$\leftarrow$ defout $- 1$

Apart from the environment, no process may issue a message unless it has received one and has not returned to its initial state defined by defin = defout = 0; this means that a message can be sent only if it does not invalidate the predicate

defin = 0 $\Rightarrow$ defout = 0

which states that a process cannot become active (and therefore send messages in its turn) unless it has received one or more messages. Further, sending an acknowledgement signal must not invalidate the predicate, a condition that ensures that when P_i sends its last signal, giving defin = 0, it will have received all the signals corresponding to the messages it has sent and therefore defout = 0.

As the deficit counters are either positive or zero and the sending of a signal by P_i decrements $defin_i$, the condition that the predicate must always hold requires that the sending of a signal is subject to the condition [HOA 69]

defin $- 1 \geqslant 0$ **and** (defin $- 1 = 0 \Rightarrow$ defout = 0)

which simplifies to

defin > 1 **or** (defin $= 1$ **and** defout = 0)

2.3 The algorithm

Having explained the principle of the algorithm we can now give the formal expression. Each process carries, in addition to the two counters, two variables, one representing its parent in the spanning tree of the graph of processes (that is, the source of the first message that it receives) and the second a set in which it records the identities of the other processes from which it has received messages. Thus for any P_i we have:

> variables defin, defout: **integer** 0, . . ., nbmax **initialized** 0;
> parent: 1, . . ., n
> others: **bag of** 1, . . ., n;

(**bag** in this last declaration indicates that any element can occur several times; this makes it possible to express the fact that a pair of processes can have several messages in transit at a given time, the acknowledgement signals not yet having been sent).

The program text for P_i is given in terms of the sending and receiving of messages and signals.

```
when received (message, expd) from expd do
        if defin = 0 then parent ← expd else others ← others + expd;
        end if;
        defin ← defin + 1;
        end do;
        received (signal, expd) from expd do
        defout ← defout − 1;
        end do;
when send (message, i) to j
        possible only (defin ≠ 0);
        do defout ← defout + 1;
        send (message, i) to j;
        end do;
wish send (signal)
        possible only (defin > 1 or (defin = 1 and defout = 0));
        do if defin = 1 then send (signal, i) to parent;
                      else oth ← an element of (others);
                            others ← others − oth;
                            send (signal, i) to oth;
        end if;
        defin ← defin − 1;
        end do;
```

2.4 Comments on the algorithm, proof of validity

The diffusing computation takes place over the set of processes but the check for termination is made on a spanning tree of the associated graph.

When the computation is completed there is no more activity in the processes and neither messages nor signals are circulating on the communication channels; further, no process is able to send any more messages or signals. It can therefore be concluded that for all processes P_i apart from the environment

defin $\geqslant 0$ **and** defout $\geqslant 0$ **and**
defin > 1 **or** (defin $= 1$ **and** defout $= 0$)

which simplifies to

defin $= 0$ **or** (defin $= 1$ **and** defout > 0)

For the environment process (the root of the spanning tree) which has no ancestors

defin $= 0$ **and** defout $\geqslant 0$

It follows that when the computation is completed

$$\forall\ P_i\text{: defin}_i \leqslant \text{defout}_i \tag{1}$$

so that, since neither messages nor signals are in transit

$$\sum_{P_i \in G} \text{defin}_i = \sum_{P_i \in G} \text{defout}_i \tag{2}$$

Finally, we have from (1) and (2) that at the end of the computation

$$\forall\ P_i\text{: defin}_i = \text{defout}_i$$

and for the environment process defin $= 0 =$ defout.

Thus the conclusion is that if the diffusing computation is completed the environment returns to its initial state. [DIJ 80] gives a proof of the converse: pseudo-terminations are not detected, so that if the environment returns to its initial state it can be concluded that the computation is completed.

The principle of the diffusing computation, with the check for completion by means of a tree structure, has been taken up by many researchers and applied to many other problems; for example, detection of deadlocks (the algorithm of [CHA 83] given in the previous chapter), termination of programs written in CSP [FRR 82, MIS 82a], distributed algorithms on graphs [CHA 82, MIS 82b]. We felt it important to present the technique in the context of the problem that gave rise to it, and have therefore given the treatment of [DIJ 80].

3 TERMINATION ON A RING: ALGORITHM OF DIJKSTRA, FEIJEN AND VAN GASTEREN [DIJ 83]

3.1 Assumptions

We are concerned with detecting the termination of a set of processes whose intercommunication can have any topology whatever; and such that a passive process can be reactivated only by receipt of a message from one of the other processes and, of course, only active processes can send such messages. We assume that communication is instantaneous and that no messages are lost: we shall see in the next section how Misra's algorithm [MIS 83] dispenses with the assumption of instantaneousness.

For the purpose of the detection, a ring structure is imposed on the processes: this has nothing to do with the topology of the communications links required by the calculation for which the set is intended, but is an abstraction necessitated by the detection procedure. The processes are arranged on this ring in the order P_0, P_1, P_2, . . ., P_{n-1}, P_0 and communication for this purpose is unidirectional between neighbours, that is from P_i to P_{i-1}.

The detection procedure is initated by a single process, say P_0.

3.2 Principle of the algorithm

This is simple, involving a token that circulates on the ring. The token is launched by P_0 when it is passive; P_0 sends it to P_{n-1} which sends it on to P_{n-2} only if (and when) it in turn is passive, and so on.

The problem that arises is that a passive process P_i that receives the token and passes it on to P_{i-1} may be reactivated by a message from a process that has not yet been visited by the token, and indeed may itself reactivate other processes that were passive when they received the token. To deal with this, and therefore to avoid recording psuedo-terminations, the token is given a 'colour' – it can be either black or white: initially it is white and its colour can be changed by a process according to a rule we shall explain; if it makes a complete turn of the ring and is white at the end of the journey then this shows that the check computation is completed.

3.3 Actions at a site

Fixing attention on the site (process) P_i, the token travels in the sequence P_0, P_{n-1}, P_{n-2}, . . ., P_i; consider the instant at which it has arrived at P_i, the previous processes being passive and the token remaining white. Suppose a process P_j with $j < i$ (meaning that P_j has not yet been visited by the token) sends a message to P_k, where $k > j$; P_j will not know where the token is at this instant and in particular will not know whether or not it has visited P_k and therefore whether or not the message has reactivated a passive process that has been observed to be passive. P_j must therefore record this possibility of reactivation, and for this purpose each process, whether active or passive, is given a colour, black or white again, with the rule that every process is white initially and becomes black only when it sends a message to a process whose identity number is greater than its own. The rule for the token colour is then that if the receiving process is white it passes the token without changing its colour, whilst if it is black it passes on a black token. (This can be summarized by saying that a white token can be transmitted only as a result of a white process receiving a white token; in all other cases a black token is transmitted.)

The effect of these rules is that P_0 detects the termination by receiving a white token when it also is white; if both conditions are not fulfilled the check is not completed and P_0 initiates another detection.

3.4 The algorithm

We give the text for the detection procedure associated with P_i, in terms of the events at that site. These events are the issue and receipt of messages and the waiting for messages; the messages concern either the distributed calculation or the detection of the termination: the first are denoted by (message, m) where m represents the content of the message, in the second by (token, ct) where ct is the colour of the token, black or white.

There are the following declarations for each process P_i:

```
constant  my_number:   value i;
variables state:        (active, passive) initialized active
          col_proc:     (black, white)    initialized white;
          col_tok       (black, white)
          tok_pres:     boolean    initialized F;    (i ≠ 0)
```

It is assumed that initially all the processes are active and of colour white: in fact, any initial colouring can be chosen (cf. [DIJ 83]). The variable tok_pres is used to record whether or not the token is present in the process; if it is, col_tok records its colour. At most one of the tok_pres variables can be T at any one time, and initially this is the one associated with P_0.

The text is as follows; all the operations on the process identifiers are performed modulo n.

```
when received (message, m) do state ← active;
                      end do;
        sent (message, m) to j
                      do if my_number < j then col_proc ← black;
                      end if;
                      send (message, m) to j;
end do)
        recieved (token, ct)      from i+1
                      do tok_pres ← T;
                      col_tok ← ct;
                      if my_number = 0 then
                              if col_proc = white and col_tok = black then
                                      termination detected else
                                      relaunch detection;
                                      end if;
                      end if)
               end do;
        sent (token, ct) to i−1
```

```
possible only state = passive and tok_pres;
    do if col_proc = black then col_tok ← black;
        end if;
        tok_pres ← F;
        send (token, col_tok) to i−1;
        col_proc ← white;
    end do;
waiting (message, m) or end do state ← passive;
        end do;
```

It should be noted that the messages concerned with checking for termination (those of type token) can travel only on the ring, and only in one direction: a message issued by P_i cannot be sent to any other process than P_{i-1}. This restriction does not apply to those of the type message: the routing of these is determined by the needs of the calculation for which the distributed algorithm is designed, and whose termination is the object of the detection procedure.

3.5 Disadvantages: Topor's algorithm [TOP 84]

This algorithm is interesting on account of its simplicity. [DIJ 83] develops it in a sequence of steps that starts from an invariant expressing the global state of the set of communicating processes and introduces first the token, then the token colour and finally the process colour; by this means the initiating process P_0 is enabled to form a reliable image of the global state, so far as termination is concerned. Whilst this certainly gives it some importance from a didactic point of view, it suffers from three major disadvantages. First, the ring topology required for the checking is superimposed on the topology of the communications system of the original algorithm, and this can require extra channels to be provided. Next, one process, P_0, plays the privileged role of initiating the procedure and finally detecting the termination; this introduces an asymmetry into the processes which can prove fatal if P_0 fails. Finally, the assumption of instantaneous transmission of messages can imply too heavy demands of parallelism, to realize this instantaneousness in an implementation.

Topor's algorithm overcomes the first of these disadvantages; his development starts from an invariant in a way similar to that of [DIJ 83] but uses a tree rather than a ring structure for the checking procedure. This is a spanning tree of the graph formed by the processes and their communication channels; the process represented by the root of the tree plays a special role: it initiates the detection procedure by sending tokens to its descendants, who then send tokens to their descendants and so on until the leaves are reached, which then return coloured tokens.

The algorithm that we describe next does not suffer from any of the above defects.

4 MISRA'S ALGORITHM [MIS 83]

4.1 Basis and assumptions

This algorithm makes no assumptions whatever about the topology of the communications channels, nor about the transit times of the messages. Its only assumptions are that no messages are lost and that messages are always received in the order in which they are sent.

As before, termination means that all the processes are passive and no messages are in transit. To detect this, Misra again uses a token in a way similar to that of [DIJ 83] just described. We have seen that the record provided by the token of having visited all the processes and found them all to be passive is not strong enough evidence of the termination of the algorithm, for processes can be reactivated and messages can be in transit. Consider the particular case in which the interprocess communication channels form a ring; the token can now state with certainty that the calculation has terminated if after a complete tour of the ring it can confirm that every process has remained permanently passive since the last visit. Since messages cannot overtake one another, between any two consecutive visits of the token any messages issued by its predecessor that were in transit after the first visit must have been received; so if the token makes two complete turns round the ring and records passiveness of all the processes at the completion of each, the additional deduction can be made that no messages are in transit and that therefore the calculation has indeed terminated.

Two problems have to be solved before an algorithm based on this principle can be constructed: a way must be found for recording the fact that a process has remained permanently passive since the previous visit of the token, and the constraint of a ring topology must be removed.

4.2 The token in Misra's algorithm

As in the previous algorithm, the first of these problems can be solved by giving 'colours' to the processors. When a process becomes active it becomes black, and the token when visiting it changes it to white on leaving; thus if the token finds a process white on arrival it knows that this has remained passive since the last visit. Initially all the processes are black; if the token has visited them all and found them all to be black, it can conclude that the calculation has terminated.

It will be seen that the emphasis is now on the behaviour of the token, that all the processes behave identically and that there is no process P_0 with a special role. Any process can start a detection procedure by launching a token, and can label this with its own identity so as to avoid confusion with any tokens issued by other processes.

The solution to the second problem, that of making any communications topology admissible, is simple. The token must visit every process and must be certain that there are no more messages in transit, and for this it must traverse every arc of the network formed by the processes and their channels of communication. Suppose this network is fully connected; then there is a cycle that includes every arc of the network, traversed at least once, and it is sufficient to replace the ring by such a cycle. The algorithm can in fact be extended to deal with the case in which the network is not fully connected (cf. [MIS 83]).

4.3 The algorithm

Let C denote the cycle derived as above. The token carries a value j showing that all the processes visited in traversing the last j communication channels (i.e. arcs of C) have remained passive, as shown by the fact that they were all white when the token arrived. For the cycle C, which is determined in advance, we define two functions, also determined in advance:

80

function size (*C*: cycle) **result integer**
function successor (*C*: cycle, *i*: 1, . . ., *n*) **result** 1, . . ., *n*

Here size is the number of arcs in the cycle and successor gives for each process P_i the identity of its successor on the cycle. The token has detected termination when $j = $ size (*C*).

There are the following declarations for each process P_i:

variables colour: (black, white) **initialized** black;
   state: (active, passive) **initialized** active;
   tok_pres: **boolean initialized** F
   nb: **integer initialized** 0

state and tok_press have their usual meanings; colour is associated with the process; nb records the value given to *j* (as defined above) between its reception and reissue by the process. Again the messages are of two types: message, identifying those relating to the algorithm whose termination is being investigated, and token, those relating to the checking procedure.

The text for P_i is as follows:

```
when received (message, m) do state ← active;
                              colour ← black;
                         end do;
     waiting (message, m) do state ← passive;
                         end do;
     received (token, j) do nb ← j;
                            tok_pres ← T;
                            if nb = size (C) and colour = white then
                               termination detected;
                            end if;
                        end do;
  issue of (token, j)
           possible only tok_pres and state = passive;
           do if colour = black then nb ← 0:
                          else nb ← nb + 1;
              end if;
              send (token, nb) to successor (C,i);
              colour ← white;
              tok_pres ← F;
           end do;
```

As this text shows, the fact that a process is black proves that it has received a message since the last visit of the token.

Initially any process may have the token, and this will be the only one for which tok_pres is T. This is not necessarily the process that detects the termination, for the value (*j*) carried by the token can be reset to zero by any process that has not remained passive since the previous visit.

4.4 Some comments

[MIS 83] gives a proof that the algorithm performs correctly, that is, that it detects true terminations and does not report pseudo-terminations. It is easily generalized to deal with a communication network that is not fully connected – this is broken into maximum sized components that are fully connected and the token made to visit these components in succession, in some suitable order.

A disadvantage is the need to define in advance a cycle that includes all the arcs of the communications graph: this can be done at compilation time for the distributed algorithm, because all the information needed is then available. There remains the problem of setting up the cycle in a distributed manner, and clearly there are two possible approaches: depth first and breadth first.

5 USE OF TIME-STAMPING: RANA'S ALGORITHM [RAN 83]

5.1 Context and assumptions

We saw in Section 1 of this chapter, where we set out the problem of termination, that we might be interested in what we called the quality of the termination: a process P_i can be said to be 'properly terminated' when not only has it become passive but in addition a certain local predicate B_i has the value T. An algorithm for detecting termination should take into account this concept of quality, and here we see the difference from detecting a deadlock: for this latter we look to see if some set of processes (not defined in advance) is passive but do not consider the quality of this passiveness (cf. Section 1.3).

Rana's algorithm takes account of quality. It is a distributed algorithm, having no dependence on a knowledge of a global state; it is symmetrical in the sense that, in contrast to the algorithms of [DIJ 80] and [DIJ 83], no process plays a special role; it assumes that the communication channels are completely reliable, meaning that no messages are lost; and it assumes that the communication mechanisms are synchronous (cf. [HOA 78, ICH 83]), meaning that the issuing and receiving of a message are organized together, these two operations obeying a protocol called the rendezvous protocol: this last assumption includes, by implication, the assumptions of finite transmission time and absence of desequencing of messages – the algorithm could be modified so as to make only these weaker assumptions.

One feature of the algorithm is that it involves the local predicates B_i; another is its use of time-stamping. This was described in Chapter 1, Section 4.2.3: each process P_i has a local clock that is incremented after each event in which it is concerned and is updated by means of messages from other processes so as to eliminate drifts between the various clocks. Each message is 'stamped' with a clock reading that records the 'time' of issue and receipt of a message, made the same by the following process which expresses the rendezvous principle: if h_i, h_j are the clocks associated with processes P_i, P_j respectively, after a communication between P_i and P_j these are reset according to the rule

$$h_i \leftarrow \max (h_i, h_j) + 1$$
$$h_j \leftarrow h_i$$

(this resetting rule appears in the text of the algorithm under the name 'hreset').

As in the case of Misra's algorithm, no restrictions are placed on the topology of the communication links between the processes of the algorithm whose termination is being tested. For the purposes of the test, the processes are treated as though linked in a cycle in which each occurs once but only once: this differs from Misra's treatment in which any process may occur more than once, to allow for the possibility that, with non-synchronous communication, messages may be in transit at any instant. Further communication channels may be needed to specify the cycle if the original graph is not fully connected.

5.2 Principle of the algorithm

This is simple; it is the same as that on which the elective algorithms described in Chapter 2 are based, in particular that of Chang and

Roberts [CHA 79] that uses the method of selective extinction of messages.

Every process P_i whose local predicate B_i (called loc_pred in the algorithm text) is T initiates a detection procedure by sending a message to its successor in the cycle of processes. When loc_pred = T this means that P_i is 'properly terminated' (P_i is necessarily passive either by termination or by waiting for messages). Consequently loc_pred = F means that P_i is 'improperly terminated', expressing these states: P_i active, or (P_i passive waiting for some message and B_i = F). If we are not interested in the quality of the termination we can take loc_pred to be T when P_i is passive and F when P_i is active.

A message concerning the detection carries two items of information relevant to that detection, a time and a number. The first is the clock reading at the process that initiated the detection at the instant of initiation, and is the instant at which its loc_pred changed to T for the last time. The second is the number of processes that have been visited by this detection message: termination is signalled by this being equal to the number of processes.

The behaviour of a process P_i on receiving a detection message depends on the value of its local predicate. If this is F it disregards the message; if it is T (and therefore P_i is 'properly terminated' and has itself issued a detection message) P_i compares the time on the message with the time it has stamped on the message that it has issued: if the received message is not the more recent of the two (shown by its time value being the smaller) P_i disregards this, if it is the more recent P_i passes it on to the successor process after having incremented the number carried.

It will be seen that the principle of selective extinction of messages is being applied here: if one or more messages are travelling around the cycle of processes, one of them is eliminated by a comparison of the times they carry. The time carried by a message is not, however, the value recording the time of issue and receipt of a message passing between two processes; it is, as the above shows, the clock reading of the process that first issued the message, at that instant. Rana's algorithm uses time-stamping only for resetting local clocks in the way described in Section 5.1, so that after any communication the clocks of the sender and the receiver show the same time. It makes explicit and normal use of the times of origination of detection messages, and these times serve to identify the messages.

5.3 The algorithm

The cycle C of processes (in which each process occurs once and only once) is defined by means of a function successor which, applied to a process P_i, gives the identity of the process that follows it in the cycle.

There are three types of message. Those concerned with the main calculation have the form (message, m) and travel along the links specified by this calculation. Those concerned with the termination detection travel around the cycle C in one direction only and have the form (detection, time, number); and detection of termination is signalled by messages of the form (terminated), also travelling around C.

There are the following declarations for each process P_i:

variables clock: 0, 1, . . . **initialized** 0
          loc_pred: boolean **initialized** F
          last_time: 0, 1, . . .
          term?:   (Y, N) **initialized** N

last_time is the time at which loc_pred last changed to T; this and clock are local variables that take strictly increasing values; term? has the value Y when the main calculation is completed and P_i is informed of this.

After each communication (in the rendezvous) the clocks of the two participating processes are reset by means of the function reset, which carries out the procedure described in Section 5.1; this is shown in the text for P_i, which follows.

```
when received (message, m) do hreset;
                             loc_pred ← F;
                      end do;
        change to T of loc_pred do last_time ← clock;
                             (β) send (detection, last_time, 1) to successor;
                             end do;
        received (detection, time, number) do hreset;
              case number = n and loc_pred = T then
           begin term? ← Y;
             send (terminated) to successor;
              end case;
              case number ≠ n and loc_pred = T then
           (α)   begin if time ≥ last_time then
                          send (detection, time, number + 1) to successor;
                          end if;
              end case;
```

```
                              end do;
    received (terminated) do if term? = N then
                              term? = Y;
                              send (terminated) to successor;
                          end if;
                      end do;
```

The change of loc_pred to T is conditioned by a calculation performed by P_i; when P_i becomes inactive it evaluates the local predicate B_i associated with the quality of the termination and assigns the value to the boolean loc_pred. As the algorithm shows, the information terminated can be broadcast without any need to update the clocks, the calculation then being completed.

Selective extinction occurs when a detection message with number $\neq n$ is received and either loc_pred = F (meaning that P_i is either active or 'improperly terminated') or loc_pred = time < last_time (meaning that P_i is passive and 'properly terminated') and has issued a detection message that is younger than the message received: this takes account of the fact that some messages could have been issued after the instant time.

5.4 Proof of correctness

Two things have to be proved in order to establish the correctness of the algorithm: first, that proper termination is always detected and second, that a pseudo-termination is not signalled. In proving these we follow the treatment given in [RAN 83].

Consider first the detection of proper termination. When the execution of the main algorithm is properly completed all the local predicates have the value T. Among the processes one, P_j say, will have been the last — in the order defined by the time-stampings — to have set its local predicate to T: suppose this occurred at the instant t_j. The detection message issued by P_j is therefore

(detection, t_j, 1)

All the other processes P_i ($i \neq j$) will have set their local predicates to T at instants t_i with $t_i \leq t_j$, and therefore (see the line marked α in the program text) the message from P_j will not be discarded by any other process P_i. Thus this message will make a complete turn of the cycle and return to P_j, which then detects the termination.

Next, detection of a pseudo-termination means that some process has received a message (detection, time, n) when there is still at least on predicate that has not been set to T: we show that this situation cannot arise. Let P_i be a process that has issued a message (detection, t_i, 1) and has therefore set its local predicate to T for the last time at t_i. P_i can become active again if an active process P_j makes a rendezvous with P_i, when loc_pred$_i$ is given the value F. If, before making this communication, and after incrementing the variable number, P_j received and passed on the message (detection, t_i, number), this means that P_j was in the 'properly terminated' state when it received this message (see line α again: loc_pred$_j$ = T and $t_i \geqslant$ last time). The same argument can be applied to the process that reactivated P_j and so on, arriving finally at a process P_k that communicates with a properly-terminated process and transmits the message (detection, t_i, number) after having incremented number; and further is such that it has not yet received this detection message. When P_k does receive this message it will discard it; if P_k is active, or more generally loc_pred$_k$ = F, it receives the message and does not pass it on; whilst if loc_pred$_k$ = T at that instant P_k will have issued a message (detection, t_k, 1) (line β) whose identifier t_k is greater than t_i and therefore does not pass on the message received (line α). The relation $t_k > t_i$ is guaranteed by the communication that has taken place between P_k and P_j: on receiving a detection message identified by t_i, P_j resets it local clock to a value such that

$$h_j \geqslant t_i + 1$$

and the communication between P_k and P_j ensures that

$$h_k = \max (h_k, h_j) + 1 > t_i$$

P_k was active at time t_i; we have thus proved that the time t_k at which P_k becomes properly terminated is such that $t_k > t_i$.

Finally, a detection message issued by P_i at time t_i will not return to P_i if there is a process P_k whose local predicate has the value F at t_i; and this proves the impossibility of signalling pseudo-terminations.

6 A NOTE ON SOME OTHER ALGORITHMS

The four algorithms described have been chosen for their diversity: each one has characteristics that are interesting from the point of view of methodology of design of distributed algorithms – diffusing computation, ring structure, value-carrying token, time-stamping. There are other algorithms for detecting termination, many of which are for application to programs written in the language CSP [HOA 78], one of whose features is synchronous communication; among the best known writings in this field are [FRA 80], [FRR 82] and [MIS 82]. Languages such as CSP and Ada provide a form of semantics of distributed termination, and detection algorithms are of fundamental importance in implementing them. An interesting treatment is that of [APT 84], where the distributed termination convention of a language is modelled in terms of other elements of the same language.

To conclude this chapter we must draw attention to the similarity between elective algorithms and some termination detection algorithms: these latter elect the last process that completes its task to convey the information that the distributed algorithm has terminated.

REFERENCES

[APT 84]   APT, K. R., and FRANCEZ, N., Modeling the Distributed Termination Convention of CSP, *ACM Toplas,* **6**(3) (July 1984), pp. 370–379.

[CHA 79]   CHANG, E. J., and ROBERTS, R., An Improved Algorithm for Decentralized Extrema-Finding in Circular Configurations of Processors, *Comm. ACM,* **22**(5) (May 1979), pp. 281–283.

[CHA 82]   CHANDY, K. M., and MISRA, J., Distributed Computations on Graphs: Shortest Paths Algorithms, *Comm. ACM,* **25**(11) (Nov. 1982), pp. 833–837.

(CHA 83)   CHANDY, K. M., MISRA, J., and HAAS, L., Distributed Deadlock Detection, *ACM TOCs,* **1**(2) (May 1983), pp. 144–156.

[DIJ 80]   DIJKSTRA, E. W., and SCHOLTEN, C. S., Termination Detection for Diffusing Computations, *Inf. Proc. Letters,* **11**(1) (Aug. 1980), pp. 1–4.

88

[DIJ 83]   DIJKSTRA, E. W., FEIJEN, W. H. J., and VANGASTEREN, A. J. M. Derivation of a Termination Detection Algorithm for Distributed Computation, *Inf. Proc. Letters,* **16** (June 1983), pp. 217–219.

[FRA 80]   FRANCEZ, N., Distributed Termination, *ACM Toplas,* **2**(1) (Jan. 1980), pp. 42–55.

[FRR 82]   FRANCEZ, N., and RODEH, M., Achieving Distributed Termination Without Freezing, *IEEE Trans. on Solt. Eng.,* **8**(3) (May 1982), pp. 287–292.

[HOA 69]   HOARE, C. A. R., An Axiomatic Basis for Computer Programming, *Comm. ACM,* **12**(10) (Oct. 1969), pp. 576–580.

[HOA 78]   HOARE, C. A. R., Communicating Sequential Processes, *Comm. ACM,* **21**(8) (Aug. 1978), pp. 666–677.

[ICH 83]   ICHBIAH, J. *et al.*, Reference Manual for the ADA Programming Language, *ANSI/MIL-STD 1815 A* (Jan **1983**).

[LAM 78]   LAMPORT, L., Time, Clocks and the Ordering of Events in a Distributed System, *Comm. ACM,* **21**(7) (July 1978), pp. 558–565.

[MIS 82a]   MISRA, J., and CHANDY, K. M., Termination Detection of Diffusing Computations in CSP, *ACM Toplas,* **4**(1) (Jan. 1982), pp. 37–43.

[MIS 82b]   MISRA, J., and CHANDY, K. M., A Distributed Graph Algorithm: Knot Detection, *ACM TOPLAS,* **4**(4) (Oct. 1982), pp. 678–680.

[MIS 83]   MISRA, J., Detecting Termination of Distributed Computation Using Markers, *Proc. of the 2nd annual ACM Symposium on Principles of DC, Montreal* (Aug. 1983), pp. 290–294.

[RAN 83]   RANA, S. P., A Distributed Solution of the Distributed Termination Problem, *Inf. Proc. Letters,* **17** (July 1983), pp. 43–46.

[TOP 84]   TOPOR, R. W., Termination Detection for Distributed Computations, *Inf. Proc. Letters,* **18** (Jan. 1984), pp. 33–36.

5

PROTOCOLS FOR DATA TRANSFER ·

1 INTRODUCTION

The aim of distributed algorithms for managing transfers is to ensure that information is transferred reliably between communicating processes. Some of these algorithms, called protocols when they concern communication over networks (see [MER 79], [TAN 81]), have been normalized so as to make it possible to transfer information between hardware devices of different types and origins; this normalization is achieved by introducing the idea of levels of abstraction (equivalently, layers of protocols) in such a way that precisely defined services can be offered to the using processes [ZIM 80].

We shall not consider these normalized protocols here, nor the classical protocols of the alternating bit type [BAR 69], Stenning's protocol [STE 76] or those based on acknowledgement of reception of the PAR (positive acknowledgement retransmission) type: all these are fully covered in the literature of networks or distributed systems (e.g. in [TAN 81] and [COR 81]). What we shall study are protocols specifically concerned with data transfer, actually various protocols developed in connection with the implementation of the communication language CSP [HOA 78] and one for reliable broadcasting of information. The study of such implementation protocols is important on several counts: take first the case of CSP.

If a language offered to application programmers is to include the concept of communication as one of its basic elements, some way must be found of putting this concept into action [KES 81] and the protocols that achieve this must have certain properties, both quantitative (e.g. they must not require too many messages to be exchanged) and qualitative (e.g. they must not cause deadlock in a program that was otherwise free of this). The complexity of such a protocol will in general be a function of the level of sophistication of the communication facilities offered by the language. It is important to study these questions as they apply to CSP because this language, whilst offering a simple and basic concept of communication employing the rendezvous mechanism, offers also the possibility of use in non-deterministic situations – meaning situations in which a sequential process can take into account the parallelism in its environment; this can lead to non-trivial distributed algorithms for providing the corresponding communication facilities.

In the case of information broadcasting the study is important because, quite apart from the fact that this is an essential activity in certain applications such as networks and distributed databases, it can be regarded as a basic tool in communication, making possible the use of novel methods for writing programs in terms of communicating processes. Gehani [GEH 84] has given a method for designing programs in terms of sequential processes that broadcast information.

2 PROTOCOLS FOR THE IMPLEMENTATION OF CSP

2.1 The CSP language: a short introduction

This language — it would be more correct to speak of the elements of a language — was introduced by Hoare in [HOA 78]; it takes communication between processes as a basic concept for program construction. It has had a considerable influence both on programming methodology and on the definition of new languages, for example Ada. The concepts in the language and the conciseness of its expressions make it attractive to use and, when it is used for defining implementation protocols for communication in a non-deterministic context, impose lighter conceptual and syntactic burdens than other languages.

A CSP program consists of a set of processes communicating by means of messages. The number of processes is defined statically, they execute in parallel and there are no global variables. Communication is by means of input and output commands denoted by '?' and '!' respectively. Control of communication is by means of the rendezvous — in operational terms, the first process to arrive waits for the other, whether the command is input or output, and the requesting process is explicitly designated as such. As an example, consider a pair of processes P, Q that communicate an item of information between themselves:

$$Q :: [\ldots P \; !15 \ldots]$$
$$P :: [\ldots Q \; ?x \ldots]$$

The statements $P \; !15$ and $Q \; ?x$ appearing in Q and P respectively when executed cause the value 15 to be transferred from Q to P and assigned to the variable x of P; this is equivalent to the synchronized execution $P.x := Q.15$.

A non-deterministic (or *alternative*) control structure allows a process to make a random choice of a communication operation from among a number of possibilities. Thus consider the following process P, where $*[\ldots]$ denotes a loop:

$$P :: *[\; Q \; ?a \qquad \rightarrow S1$$
$$\qquad \Box a < b; \; R \; ?b \rightarrow S2$$
$$\qquad]$$

The process P consists of two actions $S1$, $S2$ guarded by commands that include communications and a condition; the symbol $\Box$ is a separator. If $a < b$ (i.e. the condition is satisfied) P chooses one of the guards at random, executes it and continues with the corresponding one of $S1$, $S2$; if $a < b$ is found to be F then P must choose the first possibility, executing $Q?$ a and then $S1$. This is so whatever the states of Q and R so far as communication with P is concerned, and if the chosen process is not ready to communicate at that moment then P must wait until it is; no assumptions of equitability are made in connection with such choices.

In the first version of CSP, only input commands could appear in the guards, but certain types of problem can be expressed more concisely and in a more natural way if output commands are also allowed [BER 80]. A classic example is the management of a buffer: the process responsible for this will allow a new item to be placed there provided the buffer is not already full, or an item to be removed provided the buffer is not empty at the time. If the storing and removing processes are PROD and CONS respectively and the two conditions are represented by the booleans notfull, notempty the CSP text is as follows.

```
BUFF : : [buffer: array [0, . . ., 9] of element;
            nbp, nbc: integer initialize 0;
            in, out: integer initialize 0;
            notfull: boolean identical to (nbp < nbc + 10);
            notempty: boolean identical to (nbp > nbc);
            *[notfull; PROD? buffer(in) → [in ← in + 1 (mod 10);
                                           nbp ← nbp + 1]
            □ notempty; CONS! buffer(out) → [out ← out + 1 (mod 10);
                                           nbc ← nbc + 1]
            ]
        ]
```

The limitation of this version is that an output command cannot appear within a guard. This limitation makes it necessary for every action to take place in two stages; in the first, the processes involved (BUFF and CONS here) are synchronized by means of a signal and in the second the required action is performed; thus:

```
BUFF : : [⟨declarations⟩; *[notfull; PROD? buffer(in) → S1
                           □
                           notempty; CONS?()    → CONS! buffer(out); S2
                           ]
        ]
```

This separation is used in the majority of those cases in which one process acts as a server to one or more others. Conciseness and clarity are increased by allowing both input and output commands, and the logic of the computation and of the communications is made clearer, independently of the protocols that underlie the implementation. The result is achieved by separating the client/server relation into two processes with a producer/consumer relation — as PROD and CONS in the buffer example.

We now give two protocols for the implementation of this generalized version of CSP; the first assumes an hierarchical relation among the processes, the second makes no assumptions about the relations.

2.2 Silberschatz's protocol [SIL 79]

2.2.1 The principle

The roles of the two processes that enter into a communication are not symmetrical, and Silberschatz's protocol is based on this fact. The asymmetry is of the type that is found in networks where there are client processes, requiring certain services, and server processes, providing those services, and in any communication the client always has the initiative. Silberschatz uses this in a CSP program by arranging that a process never has the initiative for a communication action (whether input or output) that is specified in the guard of one of its possible choices — that is when the situation is non-deterministic.

This implementation can lead to a situation in which no member of a set of communicating processes can take the initiative for a communication that it wishes to make, so that there is a deadlock: it is important to realize that this is a consequence of the choice of implementation protocol and not of the computation being performed or of the communications between the processes themselves. To avoid this possibility, CSP programs with which the protocol would lead to such a deadlock must be rejected; it will arise when at some point in the program all the possible communications are given in the guards.

To formalize this situation we need to define the client/server relation between a pair of processes: we can write this

P1 serves P2 or P2 serves P1

The relation must be antisymmetrical, and the graph for a set of processes must have no cycles; it is one of strict ordering between the processes and can either be defined by the programmer or be set up by the compiler: in either case the compiler must check that the relation has the required properties.

2.2.2 The protocol

If processes P1, P2 are related by 'P1 serves P2', the behaviour of P2 is that of a client, having the initiative in any communication, and of P1 is that of a server, waiting for a signal from the client requesting communication.

Let P be a process that is in a relation of 'servitude' with all the processes R with which it communicates: that is, for each R, either P serves R or R serves P. P has the following declarations:

type servitude = (⟨list of processes R such that P serves R⟩);
variables canread, canwrite: **array**(servitude) of **boolean initialized** F;
       endrdv: **boolean initialized** F;
       buffer: **message**;

The type servitude for P is defined by its program text; it contains the names of all the processes with which P communicates in a guard.

Setting canread[Q] := T means that the process Q authorizes P to read Q's variable buffer: this is a communication in which Q is the sender of the message and the initiator of the communication.

Setting canwrite[Q]:= T means that P is allowed to write in the variable buffer belonging to Q: here Q is again the initiator but now the receiver of the message.

The local variables of P are set to T by messages from the initiator Q.

The variable endrdv of Q is set to T by P to show that the transfer is completed and therefore the rendezvous ended.

Following [SIL 79] we give the text of the protocol in terms of certain abstract communication primitives, so as to have a simple expression; the primitives are easily implemented as exchanges of typed messages. They are:

put (p, m):   put the message m in the buffer of process p
get (p, m):   get the content of the buffer of p and put it in m
signal (p, v): set to T the boolean V of p
wait (c):   wait until condition c is T

We give the two protocols, corresponding to the two directions of transfer, for the communicating processes P, Q where Q is the initiator.

Transfer of data from Q (initiator) to P

P translation of $Q?a$	Q translation of $P!b$
wait (canread[Q]); get (Q, a); canread[Q] ← F) signal $(Q,$ endrdv);	buffer ← b; signal $(P,$ canread[Q]); wait (endrdv); endrdv ← F;

Transfer of data from P to Q (initiator)

P translation of $Q!a$	Q translation of $p?b$
wait (canwrite[Q]); put (Q, a); canwrite[Q] $\leftarrow$ F; signal (Q, endrdv);	signal (P, canwrite [Q]); wait (endrdv); $b \leftarrow$ buffer; endrdv $\leftarrow$ F;

In each of these protocols Q has the initiative in causing the transfer to take place, whichever its direction: that is P serves Q. In the general case P will wait for there to be communication commands in several guards at the same time and if the conditions are such that several choices are open will make one at random. In the following example P either waits to receive a transfer from some one of a set of processes Q_i or to make a transfer to some one of a set R_i, all choices being made in a non-deterministic manner:

$$
\begin{aligned}
P :: \ [Q_1?a \quad &\leftarrow S1 \\
\square \ \ldots \\
\square \ Q_n?a \quad &\leftarrow Sn \\
\square \ R_1!b \quad &\leftarrow T1 \\
\square \ \ldots \\
\square \ R_m!b \quad &\leftarrow Tm \\
]
\end{aligned}
$$

For the process P this is expressed

$$\text{servitude} = (Q_1, Q_2, \ldots, Q_n, R_1, R_2, \ldots, R_m);$$

When P arrives at this set of alternatives it waits until at least one communication is possible before choosing arbitrarily among the possibilities. This is expressed formally as follows:

```
wait ( ⋁      canread[Q_i] ⋁   ⋁    canwrite[R_i]);
       1≤i≤n               1≤i≤m
choose a process Z such that canread[Z] ⋁ canwrite[Z];
execute protocol corresponding to choice made;
```

The implementation of the communications primitives put, get, signal is easily done by means of exchanges of messages of three types: message, request and modifbool, which are used respectively to transmit messages, to request messages and to inform of the modification of booleans. This use is as follows, where the boolean b is initialized to F:

Function to be implemented	Commands in requesting process	Commands in receiving process
put(p,m)	**send**(message,m) **to** p;	(message,m) **do** buffer $\leftarrow m$; $b \leftarrow$ T; **end do**;
get(p,m)	$b \leftarrow$ F;	(request, q) **do send**(message, buffer) **to** q; **end do**;
	send(request, q) **to** p; **wait**(b); $b \leftarrow$ F; $m \leftarrow$ buffer;	
signal(p,v)	**send**(modifbool, v) **to** p;	(modifbool, v) **do** $v \leftarrow$ T; **end do**;

Each process is of course provided with the facilities associated with the reception of messages, independently of these primitives.

We have confined our discussion of these protocols to the case where one of the communication actions (! or ?) is in a guard and the other is not, and the implementation does not allow both to be in the guards; we next give a protocol that does allow this, and which therefore does not rely on any asymmetry. The case in which both the communication actions are outside the guards — so that, theoretically, either process has the initiative — can be dealt with by giving one the actions of the initiator protocol and the other the complementary actions.

2.3 Bernstein's protocol [BER 80]

2.3.1 Assumptions

This protocol makes the same assumption of no loss of messages as does Silberschatz's but differs fundamentally from that protocol in that it places no restriction on the way in which the communication between the participating processes can be expressed: both the required actions can now be in the guards of the choices offered.

This is an important feature because it removes the need for the servitude relation required by Silberschatz's protocol. To illustrate this we consider the following example given by Bernstein.

A set utl(i) of n user processes is performing a computation in which any process can need a certain service, and any of a set svr(j) of m server processes can provide this service. Thus any of the n processes utl(i) can send a request for this service to one of the server processes and any of the m processes svr(j) can receive such a request. An elegant formal expression of this situation can be constructed by putting the complementary communication actions of input and output in the guards of the alternatives:

[utl(i) : : ⟨computation⟩ [svr(1)! request → (server ← 1)
　　　　　　　　　　　　□ . . .
　　　　　　　　　　　　□ svr(m)! request → (server ← m)];
　　　　　　　　　　　　svr(server)? reply;
　　　　⟨computation⟩
　　　　]
[svr(j) : : *[utl(1)? request → ⟨service⟩; ult(1)! reply
　　　　　　　　□ . . .
　　　　　　　　□ utl(n)? request → ⟨service⟩; utl(n)! reply
　　　　　　]
]

The syntax of CSP allows this to be written concisely as follows:

utl(i) : : [⟨computation⟩;*[(j:1, . . ., m); svr(j)! request → (server
　　　　　　　　　　　　　← j)];
　　　　　　　　　　　　svr(server)? reply;
　　　⟨computation⟩;
　　　]

and

svr(j) : : *[(i:1, . . ., n); utl(i)? request → ⟨service⟩; utl(i)! reply]

Bernstein's paper gives other examples of this type of use of the input and output commands.

2.3.2 Principles

Suppose every process P_i of the set in question is in one or other of the states 'active', 'waiting'. When P_i arrives at a set of choices it goes into the state waiting, chooses a guard whose boolean is T and sends a request for communication to the process P_j referred to in this guard, asking P_j if it is in the state waiting for a communication concerning P_i. If when P_j receives this message it is waiting with a request for P_i it replies Y (yes) and passes into the state active; otherwise (meaning that P_j either is active or does not wish to communicate with P_i) it replies N (no), when P_i chooses another boolean that is T; if there are none, P_i remains waiting.

To ensure that all possibilities are dealt with, the case must be considered in which the request from P_i to P_j arrives after P_j has entered into similar consultations on its own behalf, that is, has sent a similar request to P_k and is waiting for a reply Y or N. Two courses are open. For one, P_j can wait for the reply from P_k before replying to P_i; but if P_k on its part has made a similar request to P_i it cannot reply to P_j – which cannot reply to P_i – which cannot reply to P_k, and we have the classic deadlock situation: so this is not satisfactory.

The other course is that P_j sends a 'hold' reply to P_i in the form of a message 'busy' which will cause P_i to repeat its original request some time later. But this also is unsatisfactory because if the same situation arises as just described, with each of P_i, P_j, P_k wishing to communicate with the next, there is nothing to prevent each process in turn sending a request to its successor, replying busy to its predecessor and then, receiving busy from its successor, repeating the cycle over again.

The way out of this difficulty is to introduce a third state for the processes and a relation that puts them in strict order. So far as communication is concerned a process becomes a three-state automaton: it is 'active' when it has set up a connection with another process or is performing some processing that is not in a guard, it is 'enquiring' when it is waiting for a reply Y, N, or busy to a request it has issued and it is 'waiting' if it has not had a reply Y from any of the processes, named in the guards, to which it has sent requests. To avoid the deadlock just described, if P_i in the state enquiring receives a request from P_j it replies Y if its last request concerned P_j and N otherwise; if P_i is in any other state at that instant it replies busy if $i < j$ but delays replying if $i > j$. P_j cannot continue its attempt to enter into a communication until it has received a reply from P_i, so if P_i does not reply the circular deadlock cannot occur. The deadlock considered here is a consequence of the way in which the communications are implemented and is prevented by the ordering of the processes.

2.3.3 The protocol

As we have just stated, in this protocol a process P_i can be in any one of the three states, with respect to communication, defined by the type

type procstate = (active, enquiring, waiting)

with the rules governing change of state as given in Section 2.3.2.

Four types of message are used; if P_i, P_j are the source and destination respectively of a message, these are:

(a) (request, typecom, i, j) P_i informs P_j of its wish to make a communication of type typecom, which specifies the direction of the desired transfer (P_i to P_j or P_j to P_i) and the type of the data to be transferred.

(b) (busy, i, j) P_i informs P_j that it cannot give a definite reply to P_j's request for communication: such a message is sent only if $i < j$, otherwise P_i delays its response to P_j's request. The message will cause P_j to repeat its request later unless it has found another partner for the communication in the meantime.

(c) (Y, i, j) P_i informs P_j that it agrees to enter into the communication.

(d) (N, i, j) P_i informs P_j that it will not enter into the communication.

In order to express its behaviour each P_i must be provided with local data structures. When P_i reaches a set of choices it first sets up a list listcom of the possible communications specified in the guards; each element of this list consists of a number identifying the process concerned, the direction of transfer and the type of the data to be transferred: thus the type of an element is (1, 2, ..., n, typecom). In addition to this list P_i maintains two arrays, both of the same type: 'delayed' containing the couples (j, v) where j is the number of a process that has sent a request to P_i and to which P_i has delayed its reply; and 'repeat' containing the couples

(j, v) where j is the number of a process that has replied 'busy' to a request from P_i.

Finally, there are the following declarations for each P_i:

type typecom = (direction of transfer, type of data to be transferred);

variables state: (active, enquiring, waiting) **initialized** active;
listcom: **list of** (1, . . ., n, typecom) **initialized** $\emptyset$;
delayed, repeat: **set** (1, . . ., n, typecom) **initialized**, $\emptyset$;
j: 1, . . ., n;
v: typecom;

The behaviour is now as follows. When P_i reaches a set of choices it sets up the list listcom, using those guards whose boolean expressions are T; selects an element of this list by means of the function next (which takes the first element of the list), stores this element in (j, v) and sends the message (request, v, i, j) to P_j. P_i then passes into the state enquiring and waits for a reply to this request; if it receives a message during this waiting period several possibilities arise, according to the type of that message:

(a) (Y, j, i): this establishes the communication with P_j; P_i passes to active.

(b) N, j, i): P_i continues its questioning, see (g) below.

(c) (busy, j, i): P_i puts (j, v) in repeat and continues as in (g).

(d) (request, v', j, i) where v' is complementary to v, meaning that one represents a sending and the other the receiving of data of the same type — the boolean function compatible ((i, v), (j, v')) is used to test for this: P_i replies (Y, i, j) to establish the communication and passes to active.

(e) (request, v', k, i) where $k \neq j$ and (k, v') defines a communication that is incompatible with those of listcom: P_i replies (N, i, k).

(f) (request, v', k, i) where $k \neq j$ and (k, v') defines a communication that is compatible with those of listcom: if $k > i$, P_i replies (busy, i, k), otherwise it delays its reply and puts (k, v') in delayed.

(g) To continue its questioning P_i takes another element from listcom and proceeds as before. If listcom has been exhausted but there are still elements in delayed, P_i takes an element (k, v') from this, sends (Y, i, k) to P_k and sends (N, i, l) to all other processes l in delayed. If delayed is empty P_i proceeds in the same way with repeat, and when both are empty passes to waiting.

(h) If P_i is active it replies (N, i, k) to any process P_k that requests a communication.

(i) If P_i is waiting it replies (Y, i, k) to the first process P_k that requests a compatible communication, (N, i, k) to any request that is incompatible.

The text for P_i is as follows

```
when set of choices reached do construct listcom; delayed ← 0; repeat ← 0;
                    (j, v) ← next (listcom)
                    send (request, v, i, j) to j;
                    state ← enquiring; end do;
received (Y, j, i) do state ← active;
                    ⟨communication between Pᵢ, Pⱼ established⟩ end do;
received (N, j, i) do (continue questioning); end do;          [see below]
received (busy, j, i) do repeat ← repeat ∪ {(j, v)};
                    (continue questioning); end do)
received (request, v', k, i) do
        case state = active then send (N, i, k) to k;
            state = waiting then if (∃(k, v) ∈ listcom and compatible ((k,v),
            (i,v'))
                        then begin send (Y,i,k) to k; state ← active; end
                        else send (N,i,k) to k end if;
            state = enquiring then
            case j = k and compatible ((j,v),(i,v')) then begin
                            send(Y,i,k) to k; ( state ← active; end;
                    j ≠ k and ∄ (k,v) ∈listcom: compatible ((k,v),(i,v')) then
                        send (N, i, k) to k;
            j ≠ k and ∃ (k, v) ∈listcom and compatible ((k,v),(i,v')) then
                        if k > i then send (busy,i,k) to k
                                    else delayed ← delayed (k, v) end if;
                    end case;
            end case;
    end do;
```

As this text shows, the protocol acts like a finite state automaton that controls the way in which the process sets up its communications. Notice that the process does not store any information about the state of its potential correspondents, but simply sends out requests to find if communication is possible at any given instant.

The section abbreviated to (continue questioning) is as follows:

```
if listcom not exhausted then begin (j,v) ← next (listcom);
                              send (request,v,i,j) to j; end;
   else if delayed ≠ ∅ then begin (k,v) ← next (delayed);
                              delayed ← delayed − {(k,v)};
                              send (Y, i, k) to k;
                              ∀ j: (j,x) ∈ delayed do send (N,i,j) to j; end do;
                              state ← active; end;
   else if repeat ≠ ∅ then begin (k,v) ← next (repeat); repeat ← repeat − {(k,v)};
                              send (request, v,i,k) to k; end;
         else state ← waiting;
   end if;
```

2.3.4 Importance and limitations of Bernstein's protocol

In Section 2.3.2 we pointed out that an implementation protocol
may produce a deadlock in a set of communicating processes that
would otherwise be free of this possibility; and that this could
result from either of two causes, according to the type of control
chosen: every process halted and waiting for a reply to a request,
or what may be called 'active waiting' with each process trapped
in the loop – issue of a request, receipt of a reply 'busy', issue of
a request, ... Bernstein's protocol uses both types of control but
arranges matters so that it is not possible for all the processes to
be either waiting for a reply or looping as described, at the same
instant. This is achieved by using the strict ordering imposed on
the processes to ensure that one will always give a response that
will enable its questioner to proceed. Thus the protocol will not
introduce a risk of deadlock.

With regard to starvation of processes, however, the position is
quite different. For example, suppose three processes P_1, P_2, P_3
wish to communicate in the way shown below, and afterwards to
continue the computation:

$$P_1 :: *[P_2!v1 \quad \leftarrow \langle comp \rangle]$$
$$P_2 :: *[P_1? \; x2 \leftarrow \langle comp \rangle$$
$$\quad \quad \Box P_3!v2 \quad \leftarrow \langle comp \rangle$$
$$\quad \quad]$$
$$P_3 :: *[P_2? \; x3 \leftarrow \langle comp \rangle]$$

Depending on the speed with which messages are transmitted
and the order in which requests for communication are issued, it
is possible for P_2 and P_3 to be in constant communication with
each other, so that P_1 is held permanently in the state waiting.

Thus P_1 is starved: it is always wishing to communicate with P_2 and although the communication is possible it is never chosen by the protocol. The definition of the CSP language (cf. [HOA 78]) includes no assumptions concerning the equitability of the communications, so in a sense Bernstein's protocol gives a correct implementation; but equitability could have been guaranteed without contravening the rules of the language.

2.4 Other protocols

A number of different implementation protocols are studied and classified in [PLR 84]. Some of these assume a hierarchy among the processes and as a consequence can be more or less restrictive; thus Van de Snepscheut [VDS 81] assumes a tree structure, whilst Silberschatz in the protocol we described (Section 2.2) assumes only a cycle in the graph. In Schneider's protocol [SCH 82] every process carries a copy of a centralized control, so that many messages are needed in the implementation. For a distributed solution based on local states there are the Bernstein protocol that we have described and that due to Buckley and Silberschatz [BUC 83]; the latter, a generalization of Bernstein's treatment, is free of the risks of deadlock and starvation but is cumbersome and complicated.

3 METHODS FOR RELIABLE BROADCASTING OF MESSAGES

3.1 The problem

If facilities for message broadcasting are built into a distributed system and are available to all the processes then nothing more is needed; but whilst local networks of the Ethernet type [MET 76] provide these, many systems provide nothing more than primitives for sending and receiving messages between two points. If broadcasting is necessary to the applications that use such a system it must be provided by adding a special layer of protocol. This is a simple matter when the constituent processes and the communication links are reliable — that is, the processes do not break down and the links neither lose nor corrupt messages nor deliver them out of sequence: the process wishing to broadcast a message merely sends a copy to every other process. The problem is much more difficult if the system is not reliable in this sense; it is solved in the protocol due to Schneider, Greis and Schlichting [SCH 84] which we describe later.

3.2 Context of the problem, assumptions

We assume that the communication system is reliable (messages neither lost nor corrupted nor desequenced) but processes can fail; and that any process can send a message to any other process that has not failed. The topology of the physical communication links can be anything, but must allow for the possibility of up to k processes failing simultaneously and therefore must provide $k+1$ independent channels between every pair of processes. With the configuration

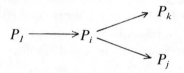

with only a single link between P_1 and P_i, a failure of P_i will prevent there being any communication between P_1 and P_j or P_k.

When a process fails all its activity ceases and the other processes are informed. The implementation protocols for the communication system ensure its reliability and the monitoring of failures.

3.3 Principles of protocol

The first necessity is to define a strategy for the routing of a broadcast message m, issued by a process P, to all the other processes; what is chosen here is a spanning tree with P as root, with the function succ(Q) used to give all the successors in the tree to a subset (Q) of processes.

Messages of two types are exchanged in a broadcast: message and ack; these carry the identifier i of the sender, a sequence number nbseq and, in the case of message, the content m of that message; the sequence numbers enable the messages sent by a given process to be identified. Reliability of the broadcast protocol is defined by the statement that if m is the last message sent by a process P (which has therefore remained operational during this broadcast) then if one operational process has received m all such processes have received or will receive m.

The principle is as follows, there being two cases to consider according as the broadcasting process P_i does or does not fail during the broadcast. Take first the second possibility. Applying the principle of the diffusing computation method (Chapter 1, Section 4.2.1), P_i broadcasts the message to its successors in the tree of which it is the root, say succ($\{i\}$), and waits until it has received their acknowledgements. A process P_j that receives this message broadcasts it in turn to its sucessors succ($\{j\}$) and does not reply to P_i until it has received all its acknowledgements. If any process P_k fails, all the others are informed. Consider now, in the tree growing from P_i, first a failed process P_k, then the parent of P_k, then the parent of this parent if it (P_k's parent) also has failed and so on until an operational process is reached: call this P_j. Whether or not P_j has sent the message to P_k, it will not receive the corresponding acknowledgement, so it sends the message to succ ($\{k\}$) and waits for their acknowledgements. Every process knows the complete structure of the tree growing from P_i and the failure of a process is equivalent to a reconfiguration of this tree, which is always possible because of the assumption of the number of independent paths provided between every pair of processes.

Take now the case in which P_i does fail, which itself falls into two cases. If the failure occurs before any of P_i's successors has received the message then the broadcast ends. If at least one process has received the message, it will have been informed of the failure and can act as though it were P_i; and as the same can apply to every member of succ($\{i\}$) that has received the message there must be some means provided for ensuring that the same message sent out on P_i's account by different successors of P_i is received only once; this is where the sequence number nbseq is used to detect multiple receptions of the same message.

A further assumption we make is that every process numbers the messages it broadcasts in strict sequence: that is, it does not send out a message with number (nbseq + 1) until after it has received all the acknowledgements for that with nbseq.

3.4 Schneider, Gries and Schlichting's protocol [SCH 84]

We follow [SCH 84] in giving the protocol as it applies to the broadcasting of messages by a single process (or site) P_i with the topology of the process communications known to all the (operational) members of succ($\{i\}$). If any processes fail, the topology can be reconfigured because each process is informed of the failure(s) and there are sufficient channels.

We have defined the two types of message; formally, these are

(message, m, sequence-number, sender)
(ack, sequence-number, sender)

where the first carries the message and the second the acknowledgement.

There are the following declarations for each P_j, where $j \neq i$:

variables sendto, ackof, ackto, fail: set of 1, 2, . . ., n, **initialize** $\emptyset$;
msg: structure (m, seqnum) **initialize** (nil, 0);
role: 1, 2, . . ., n **initialize** j;

These variables have the following meanings:

sendto: the set of processes to which the current message is to go

ackof: the set from which P_j is waiting for acknowledgement of the last message from P_i in which broadcast P_j was involved

ackto: the set of processes which have all sent the same message to P_j and to which P_j must send an acknowledgement

fail: specifies the set of failed processes; this is updated by the communications system

msg: carrier for the last message broadcast by P_i – only the sequence number of the message and the sender's identifier are kept.

role: identifier of the process whose role has been taken over by P_j at that instant; a process normally plays its own role, taking over that of the broadcaster P_i only when informed of the failure of the latter.

When P_j receives a message it compares the sequence number of this with that of the last message in the broadcasting of which it has been concerned. If the former is 'older' than the latter (i.e. earlier in the sequence) P_j sends an acknowledgement immediately; if the two messages are the same it records that it must send an acknowledgement, but delays this until it has sent the new message to all its (P_j's) successors and received their acknowledgement — it cannot respond immediately because it may not have completed the broadcasting of this message. If the new message is the younger this means that the broadcasting of the previous message from P_i is completed: P_i cannot make a new broadcast until after it has received all the acknowledgements needed to guarantee the completion of the previous one. If P_j must still send acknowledgements concerning this previous message it does so and then takes part in the broadcasting of the new message. All this is expressed as follows.

```
when received (message, m, ns, k) do
    case ns < msg.seqnum then send (ack, ns, j) to k end
    case;
    case ns = msg.seqnum then ackto ← ackto ∪ {k} end
    case;
    case ns > msg.seqnum then begin
        ∀ p: p ∈ ackto: send (ack, msg.seqnum, j) to p;
        msg ← (m, ns);
        role ← j;
        ackto ← k;
        sendto ← succ (j);
        ackof ← ∅;
            end; end case;
        end do;
```

So long as its set sendto is not empty, P_j participates in the broadcast, sending the message msg to all the members of this set. If any process from which P_j is waiting for a response fails, and the broadcast is not yet completed, P_j takes charge of the successors of this process and sends them the message, and on receiving an acknowledgement modifies the set ackof appropriately. When P_j becomes aware of the failure of the sending process P_i, it waits until it has made all its own broadcasts and received all the corresponding acknowledgements and then takes over the role of

P_i, sending the last message received to P_j's immediate successors. Finally P_j sends the acknowledgements to the members of *ackto* when (after sending the broadcast message) it has received the corresponding acknowledgements, or when it is playing the role of P_i: it plays this role only while making these broadcasts and receiving the responses.

The text for P_j is as follows.

```
when received (message, m, ns, k) do
    case ns < msg.seqnum then send (ack, ns, k) to k end case;
    case ns = msg.seqnum then (ackto ← ackto k end case;
    case ns > msg.seqnum then begin
                    ∀ p ∈ ackto: send (ack, msg.seqnum, j) to p;
                    msg ← (m, ns);
                    role ← j; sendto ← succ ({j});
                    ackto ← {k}; ackof ← ∅;
                            end; end case;
                        end do;
    sendto ≠ ∅ do d ← element of (sendto); sendto ← sendto − {d};
                    if d ≠ j then begins endto ← sendto ∪ {d};
                            send (message, msg.m, msgseqnum, j) do d;
                        end;
                end if;
            end do;
    ackto ∩ fail ≠ ∅ do t ← ackto ∩ fail;
                    sendto ← sendto ∪ succ(t); ⟨each element of t⟩
                    ackof ← ackof − t;
                end do;
    when received (ack, ns, k) do
        if ns = msg.seqnum then ackof ← ackof − {k}; end if;
                    end do;
    i ∈ fail ∧ role ≠ i ∧ ackof = ∅ ∧ sendto = ∅ do role ← i;
                            sendto ← succ({i}); end do;
    ackto ≠ ∅ (role = i ∧ (sendto = ∅ ∨ ackof = ∅)) do
            ∀ p ∈ ackto: send (ack, msg.seqnum, j) to p;
            ackto ← ∅;                        end do;
```

The same declarations apply to the process P_i that originates the broadcst (that is, the root of the relevant spanning tree) with the addition of

nbseq: 0, 1, . . ., ∞ **initialize** 0;

which it uses to number the messages it issues. The program text for P_i is identical to that for P apart from this difference: P_i cannot both observe itself to have failed and initiate broadcasts, so the section of the P_j text from '$i \in$ fail $\cdot \wedge$ role . . .' to the end is replaced by the following:

```
when ackof = ∅ ∧ sendto = ∅ do nbseq ← nbseq + 1;
                             msg ← (newmessage, nbseq);
                             sendto ← succ ({i});
                 end do;
```

This ensures the validity of the assumption that a new broadcast can be started only when the previous one is completed.

3.5 Comments

[SCH 84] gives a proof of correctness of this protocol; it constructs a predicate that expresses the property of reliable broadcasting and shows that the value of this predicate, initially T, is conserved in the operation of the protocol.

The protocol is easily generalized to deal with the case in which every process can be a broadcaster of messages; for this, the function 'succ' used above must have two arguments, one as before and the other the identifier of the initiating process. Further, it is necessary now to take account of not just the sequence number of a message in order to identify it but of the couple ⟨sequence number, identifier of initiator⟩. A similar method was used in the Chandy, Misra and Haas algorithm for deadlock detection [CHA 83], described in Chapter 3, Section 5.

In [SCH 84] an extension to the protocol is suggested to deal with the possibility of reinstatement of a process after a failure.

In the protocol, as it has been described, each process of the set sends a given message at most once to every other member and receives from each at most one acknowledgement; so for a set of n processes, subject to possible failure, the maximum number of messages needed for the reliable broadcasting of a single message is $2n(n-1)$.

Many other protocols have been proposed for this purpose, for both local and general networks. Most provide recovery from a failure of a process other than the initiator of the broadcast by reconfiguring the spanning tree, and from a failure of the initiator by discarding its last message if this has not been received by all the other processes. The present protocol is more powerful because it ensures reliable broadcasting provided only one process has received the message; this has a considerable advantage for distributed databases, where all the copies of any item must be brought to the same value.

REFERENCES

[BAR 69] BARTLETT, K. A., SCANTLEBURY, R. A., and WILKINSON, P. T., A note on Reliable Full-Duplex Tranmission over Half Duplex links, *Comm. ACM*, **12**(5) (May 1969), pp. 260–261.

[BER 80] BERNSTEIN, A. J., Outputs guards and Non-Determinism in CSP, *ACM Toplas*, **2**(2) (Apr. 1980), pp. 234–238.

[BUC 83] BUCKLEY, G. N., and SILBERSCHATZ, A., An Effective Implementation for the Generalized Input–Output Construct of CSP, *ACM Toplas*, **5**(2) (Apr. 1983), pp. 223–235.

[CHA 83] CHANDY, K. M., MISRA, J., and HAAS, L. M., Distributed Deadlock Detection, *ACM TOCS*, **1**(2) (May 1983), pp. 144–156.

[COR 81] CORNAFION, (group name), *Systèmes Informatiques Répartis*, Dunod (1981), 368 p.

[GEH 84] GEHANI, N., Broadcasting Sequential Processes, *IEEE Trans. on SE*, **4** (July 1984), pp. 343–351.

[HOA 78] HOARE, C. A. R., Communicating Sequential Processes, *Comm. ACM*, **21**(8) (Aug. 1978), pp. 666–677.

[KES 81] KESSELS, J. L. W., The Soma: A Programming Construct for Distributed Processing, *IEEE Trans. on SE*, **7**(5) (Sept. 1981), pp. 502–509.

[MER 9] MERLIN, P M., Specification and Validation of Protocols, *IEEE Trans. on Comm.*, **27**(11) (Nov. 1979), pp. 1671–1680.

[MET 76] METCALFE, R. M. Ethernet: Distributed Packet Switching for Local Computer Networks, *Comm. ACM*, **19**(7) (1976), pp. 395–406.

[PLR 84] PLOUZEAU, N., and RAYNAL, M., Protocoles d'Implémentation du concept de Communication du langage CSP, *Rapport de Recherche, LSI, Université de Toulouse*, **3** (June 1984).

[SCH 82] SCHNEIDER, F. B., Synchronisation in Distributed Programs, *ACM Toplas*, **4**(2) (Apr. 1982), pp. 125–148.

[SCH 84] SCHNEIDER, F. B., GRIES, D., and SCHLICHTING, R. D., Fault-Tolerant Broadcast, *Science of Computer Programming*, **4**(1) (1984), pp. 1–15.

[SIL 79] SILBERSCHATZ, A., Communication and Synchronization in Distributed Systems, *IEEE Trans. on SE*, **5**(6) (Nov. 1979), pp. 542–546.

[STE 76] STENNING, W., A Data Transfer Protocol, *Computer Networks*, **1** (1976), pp. 99–110.

[TAN 81] TANENBAUM, A. S., Networks Protocols, *Computing Surveys*, **13**(4) (Dec. 1981), pp. 453–489.

[VDS 81]   VAN DE SNEPSCHEUT, J. L. A., Synchronous Communication between Asynchronous Processes, *Inf. Proc. Letters,* **13**(3) (Dec. 1981), pp. 127–130.

[ZIM 80]   ZIMMERMANN, H., OSI Reference Model – The ISO Model of Architecture for Open Systems Interconnection, *IEEE Trans. on Comm.,* **28** (Apr. 1980), pp. 425–432.

6

MANAGEMENT OF DISTRIBUTED DATA

1 INTRODUCTION

1.1 Nature of the data

The problem of managing data when they are to be used by several processes is considered in the first chapter of [RAY 86]; we shall not go into all the details here but simply summarize the main features. First, every data object – a term we shall use to indicate a data item, a set of items or a file – needs a support, meaning what is usually called a system resource; consequently, if data objects are to be used independently by several different processes the classic problems of access control arise because of the need to ensure mutual exclusion and freedom from deadlock. A third problem arises when the data objects are not independent but are related by *consistency constraints* (ESW 76]. Consider for example a pair of objects a, b related by the constraint $a = b$ that holds at the start of the processing with $a = b = i$. The relation must be checked whenever the values of a and b can be observed, that is, before and after the execution of any processing applied to them. Suppose now there are two processes

$$P1: a \leftarrow a + 1, b \leftarrow b + 1;$$
$$P2: a \leftarrow 2 * a, b \leftarrow 2 * b;$$

Each, taken separately, preserves the relation and so does not violate the constraint; but if they are executed in parallel with the interleaving as represented by

$$a \leftarrow a + 1, a \leftarrow 2 * a, b \leftarrow 2 * b, b \leftarrow b + 1$$

113

the result is $a = 2(i + 1)$, $b = 2i + 1$ and the relation $a = b$ no longer holds. No questions concerning mutual exclusion or deadlock arise in this example, so we see at once that the problems of ensuring consistency cannot be reduced to those of dealing with mutual exclusion or deadlocks. The need to preserve consistency relations, especially in the case of databases (cf. [GAR 83]) leads to the need for special rules for management of the data that are expressed by new access protocols for the processes concerned.

1.2 Distribution of data

The set of data objects used by a set of communicating processes distributed over a number of distinct sites can be treated in three different ways: centralized, with everything held at one physical location; partitioned, with the different partitions held at different sites and no item held at more than one site; and duplicated, with a copy of every item at every site. We consider these in turn.

Centralization
In this case everything takes place as though the whole system were centralized, with the site where the data are held acting as access controller for all the processes. The type of control used will vary according to the strategy chosen; it can depend on two-phase locking, ordering of accesses, certification or other techniques. The interested reader should consult [BER 81] or [BOK 84] for an excellent discussion of the subject, or works on the implementation of databases such as [GAR 83] or [ULL 82]. Here we shall deal only with distributed algorithms.

Partitioning
Here each site supports a unique subset of the data, but any consistency constraint can involve objects at different sites and any process can access objects at any of the sites. Because no object is located at more than one site this case can be reduced to the previous, centralized, case.

Duplication
The extra problem that arises here is that of ensuring that all the copies of the same object held at the different sites always have

the same value. This is a consistency problem (cf. [COR 81]), referred to as the convergence of all copies to the same value.

A distributed system can involve a combination of partitioning and duplication, leading to problems that we have described.

1.3 Problems to be discussed

For the special problems of databases we refer the reader to the works already quoted; here we shall restrict ourselves to those posed by the distribution of data and therefore concern ourselves with the relevant distributed algorithms. Thus we take up two problems: ensuring consistency of duplicated data items and developing distributed control algorithms for use with centralized databases.

2 CONSISTENCY OF DUPLICATED DATA

2.1 Context of the problem

Independently of any considerations of use by processes and preservation of internal consistency relations, we are interested here in the consistency of data items duplicated at a number of distinct sites. These can be read or written by the various processes, each executing at its own site, the reading and writing operations being performed by means of messages sent to the process controllers, each of which manages one copy of the data item in question; and all these copies must be consistent, meaning that at any instant each one must represent the same value of that item.

Two problems arise. One, ensuring, where possible, that any two copies of the same item have undergone the same history of modifications – a question of an algorithm for maintaining mutual consistency; the other, when this has not been achieved and the copies have diverged, to detect this divergence – the problem of detection of mutual inconsistency. A third problem arises when a new site is added to the system and requires up-to-date copies of all the data – the problem of initialization of a site. We shall give an algorithm for each of these problems.

2.2 Detection of mutual inconsistency: algorithm of Parker *et al.* [PAR 83]

2.2.1 The problem

Consider a network of a number of sites, at each of which is a copy of the same set of data, used by processes executing at that site and all obeying the same protocol to ensure the consistency of the various copies; then all the copies of the same item converge to the same value.

Breakdowns that may occur in the network can result in a partitioning of this into subnetworks, each of which will then proceed with its own sequence of modifications to the data held at its constituent sites. Whilst the obeying of the protocol will ensure that the data in each subnetwork remain consistent among themselves, the separation can result in divergences between the subnetworks as entities.

A network that has been partitioned as a result of one or more breakdowns may be reconstituted as a result of operations undertaken after the failures have been detected. The history can be modelled by a graph in which each node represents the group of sites that form a particular subnetwork. Suppose for example there are initially four sites $S1$, $S2$, $S3$, $S4$ constituting a single network and that the following breakdowns occur, in this order, with the following effects:

(a) separation into two subnetworks consisting of $(S1,S2)$ and $(S3,S4)$
(b) further separation into $(S1)$, $(S2,S3)$, $(S4)$
(c) repair and reconfiguration to give $(S1)$, $(S2,S3,S4)$
(d) further repair and reconfiguration to restore the original $(S1,S2,S3,S4)$.

The corresponding graph is as follows:

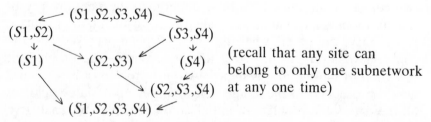

(recall that any site can belong to only one subnetwork at any one time)

Whenever the network is reconfigured two or more subnetworks are combined into one, and the question that arises is, are the copies of the same data item in different subnetworks identical or not? — and if they are not, is any one 'more up to date' than any other? If they are identical, convergence of the two (or more) sets is possible, if not they are mutually inconsistent.

2.2.2 Underlying principle of the solution

We can immediately dispose of the trivial possible method for checking the identity of the copies, that of element-by-element comparison: this can be extremely expensive, and does not give an answer to the question of whether or not there is mutual inconsistency when the copies are not identical.

The solution proposed by Parker *et al.* is based on a simple principle and enables both of the above questions to be answered. In order to detect whether two sets of copies are identical (so that in each set all copies of the same item have the same value), and, if not, whether they are compatible, it is necessary to keep a record of all the modifications made to each copy at each site. For this a vector that records this history is associated with each copy; each component of the vector corresponds to a particular site and records the number of times that site has modified the item. A copy of this vector is attached to every copy of the data item that it concerns and whenever any site makes a modification to that item this is recorded in every copy of the vector, wherever that is in the network.

Returning to the previous example of four sites initially forming a single network, let there be a copy of the item at each site. If at some later stage $S1$ has modified this once, $S2$ twice, $S3$ four times and $S4$ three times this can be represented by the vector

$$[1, 2, 4, 3]$$

So far as updating is concerned the vector will be manipulated along with the data item to which it refers; so in general the manipulation will involve the couple

$$([i_1, i_2, \ldots, i_n], \langle \text{copy of item} \rangle)$$

where the (integer) element i_k shows that site S_k has made i_k modifications to that copy of the item.

At a reconfiguration new subnetworks are formed from old and the sites that thus become members of the new subnetworks must check to find if there is any mutual inconsistency among their copies of the data. At any instant any partition of the original network constitutes an autonomous subnetwork and maintains mutual consistency within itself, and any given site belongs to only one subnetwork. It follows that the copies of the data held at the sites that participate in the formation of a new subnetwork will be identical if and only if the vectors associated with the different copies of the same item are identical: for then they represent the same history of modifications.

For the case in which the vectors are not all identical the idea of *compatibility* is introduced: a set of vectors is said to be compatible (in the sense needed here) if either all the members of the set are identical or there is one member that is greater than any of the others — 'greater' meaning that every component of the greater vector is greater than the corresponding component of any other vector. For example, for the set $V1$, $V2$, $V3$, $V4$

$$V1 = [1, 2, 4, 3]$$
$$V2 = [0, 2, 2, 3]$$
$$V3 = [1, 2, 3, 4]$$
$$V4 = [1, 2, 4, 4]$$

$\{V1, V2\}$ is a compatible set because $V1 > V2$; and in terms of the network ($S1$, $S2$, $S3$, $S4$) this means that all the modifications represented by $V2$ have been recorded by $V1$, so the copy associated with $V1$ is the 'more up to date'; the relation also expresses the fact that $V2$ represents an earlier stage in the history of modifications represented by $V1$. The vectors of $\{V1, V3\}$ are incompatible: this means that they represent different histories of modifications, and that mutual incompatibility has been detected.

Continuing, the vectors of $\{V1, V3, V4\}$ are compatible because $V4 > V3$ and $V4 > V1$; therefore $V4$ represents the 'most up to date' and includes the different modifications of both $V1$ and $V3$. Here $V1$ and $V3$ each represent a history included in that represented by $V4$. Mutual consistency has been detected here and the 'most up to date' copy identified.

2.2.3 The algorithm

Each site S_i ($i = 1, 2, \ldots, n$) has the following declarations:

> duplicated variable v_i: **array** $[1, \ldots, n]$ **of** 0, 1, $\ldots$ **initialize** 0;
> copy$_i$: **file initialize** value of file;

These two objects are managed by protocols that maintain their mutual consistency, the details of which we shall not consider here (see Section 2.3); all the variables v_i and copy$_i$ constitute an autonomous network and evolve in the same way.

The description we now give of the Parker *et al.* algorithm [PAR 83] is abstract in nature and global in the sense that it omits the messages: a fully detailed account of the behaviour of all the processes would make very heavy reading and would confuse the procedure for detecting inconsistency with the other procedures, such as those concerned with consistency and election on a subnetwork, that are needed in support of this. As before, however, the description is faithful to the event sequence.

```
when S_i modifies copy_i do v_i ← v_i[i] + 1;
                    ⟨protocols ensuring consistency of (v_j[i], copy_j) at
                     all sites S_j of network to which S_i belongs⟩
                    end do;
splitting of network do ⟨every site of every subnetwork inherits a consistent
                    couple (v, copy)⟩
                    end do;
reconfiguration of subnetworks (r_1, r_2, . . ., r_m) into single network
                    do ⟨S_{i1}, S_{i2}, . . ., S_{ik} sites forming the new network coming
                        from r_1, r_2, . . ., r_m; J = {i_1, i_2, . . ., i_k}⟩
                    if ∃j∈J:∀l∈J v_j > v_l) then
                        ⟨mutual consistency established⟩
                        (v_j, copy_j) broadcast to S_l, ∀l∈J ⟨most up-to-date copy⟩
                    else ⟨mutual inconsistency detected⟩
                        choose site S_j;
                        copy ← create new version of file;
                        v_j[j] ← v_j[j] + 1;
                        (v_j, copy_j) broadcast to S_l, ∀l∈J;
                    end if;
                    end do;
```

Problems arise in the reconfiguring of the subnetworks r_1, r_2, $\ldots$, r_m. The first need is to carry out a search for the greatest vector (in the sense defined above) among the sites taken from these networks; if there is one, v_j say, then the couple $(v_j$, copy$_j)$

is the most up to date and takes account of all the modifications; if there is no greatest vector then one site, S_j say, is chosen to create a new version based on the copies held at the sites, an action that for S_j is equivalent to modifying the file and hence to incrementing $v_j[j]$.

2.2.4 Importance and limitations of the protocol

To illustrate the working of the protocol, consider the evolution of the network given in Section 2.2.1, shown again in the figure below with the addition of the vectors associated with the copies of the subnetworks. Only one vector is given for each subnetwork since all its sites have the same value for the copy and therefore the same vector.

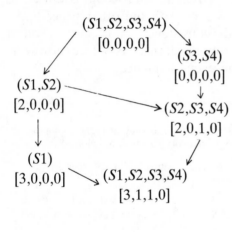

$(S1,S2,S3,S4)$ [0,0,0,0]	initial configuration
$(S3,S4)$ [0,0,0,0]	splitting $S2$ makes two modifications
$(S1,S2)$ [2,0,0,0]	
$(S2,S3,S4)$ [2,0,1,0]	splitting and reconfiguration
$(S1)$ [3,0,0,0]	
$(S1,S2,S3,S4)$ [3,1,1,0]	$S1$ – one modification $S3$ – one modification reconfiguration, inconsistency detected in $S2$ which creates a new copy

The algorithm detects inconsistency when networks are to be combined to form a single new network, and indicates which copy is to be used in the next stage. It also detects inconsistency among the copies but says nothing about how a new version is to be obtained that is consistent with those existing. There is no 'reconciliation algorithm' for the general case, because the consistent copy required depends on the semantics of the duplicated objects and of the operations performed on these. Thus if the object is simply a queue of messages to which the operations add and remove can be applied, the reconciliation of two mutually inconsistent copies is done by simply forming the union of the two sets. In some cases, however, reconciliation will prove to be impossible, and in such a case each site must record not simply the number of modifications it has made since the start but also the actual modifications made.

It is important to note that the protocol for detecting inconsistencies among copies of an object can be applied only when the operations that can be performed on these objects are monadic — that is when each operation acts on only a single object at a time. Suppose for example we have two operations op1, op2 that read two objects f, g and write into f, g respectively; and that these operations are executed in two distinct partitions, each consisting of a single site, $S1$, $S2$. Let vf, vg be the vectors associated with the objects. Consider the following graph.

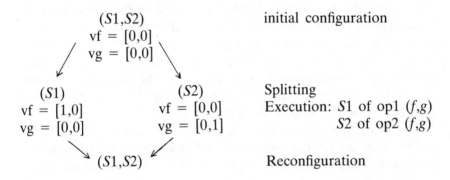

The protocol would not detect the inconsistency: whatever the copies (whose actual values are features only of the particular implementation) the result is equivalent to a sequence of the two operations

$$\text{op1 } (f,g); \text{ op2 } (f,g) \quad \text{or} \quad \text{op2 } (f,g); \text{ op1 } (f,g)$$

and no couple consisting of the two vectors (vf, vg) in either of the two subnetworks takes into account such a result or the effects of an operation on the other.

Finally, the protocol for detecting inconsistency among copies of the same object provides a necessary and sufficient condition for inconsistency under the assumption that the operations that access the duplicated objects take only a single object as argument; if this does not hold, the objects f, g can always be structured so as to make only one; thus, in the example, operation fg is possible, but not f or g alone.

2.3 Maintaining mutual consistency

2.3.1 The problem, and basis of solutions

We showed in Section 2 that the essence of this problem is finding a protocol for controlling access to the various copies of a set of data that will ensure that all the copies experience the same changes — that is, converge to the same value. All the algorithms that have been suggested as solutions to this problem are based on the same principle: there is a control procedure that allows a site to modify the copy that it holds — and at the same time, by broadcasting the modification, those at all the other sites — only if it has gained the exclusive right to do so. The principle thus involves using a mechanism for mutual exclusion among the sites; in this way a total ordering is imposed on the modifications that are made, which is the same at all sites and all the copies experience the same modifications in the same order.

The algorithm due to Thomas [THO 79] makes systematic use of the vote: a site that wishes to modify its copy must obtain the agreement of the majority before it can do so and broadcast the modification to the other sites. Other algorithms use a token (e.g. [LEL 78]); a token is associated with every file and only the holder of the token can modify the file (and broadcast the modification). A different implementation of the same principle designates, once and for all, one particular site as being responsible for a particular file, called the primary site for that file; any other site must obtain the primary site's permission to modify its copy, and again to broadcast the effect. The algorithm of Alsberg and Day [ALS 76] is of this last type.

Whilst all these algorithms are cumbersome to put into operation they have two notable qualities. One is that they attain the objective of ensuring consistency among the copies of the same object. The other is that since they are based on gaining an exclusive privilege — defined either statically in the case of the primary site or dynamically for the token or majority vote — they are not affected by partitioning of the set of sites into subnetworks, because the primary site, token or majority can be found in only one subnetwork at any one time, and therefore no site in any other subnetwork can modify its copy.

The algorithm based on the majority-vote procedure has the disadvantage that all modification is prevented if after a partitioning no subnetwork contains the majority of the sites. With the other two algorithms there must be included either an election algorithm to cover the possibility of failure of the primary site, or a regeneration algorithm in case of loss of the token. Broadcasting of the modifications to the other sites can be done with the aid of the algorithm for reliable broadcasting [SCH 84] given in Chapter 5.

We now describe an algorithm derived from Lamport's mutual exclusion algorithm [LAM 78].

2.3.2 From mutual exclusion to consistency

Lamport's algorithm uses time-stamping to impose a strict order on the requests for exclusion sent out by the various sites, the basic methodology being the distribution of the same queue to all n sites of the network. Herman and Verjus [HER 79] have shown that this algorithm can be adapted to ensuring consistency in a set of duplicated data at a number of sites by changing the requests for exclusive access to requests for modification. This is what we now describe.

Assumptions

We assume that all communication is reliable – there is neither loss nor corruption nor desequencing of messages exchanged between sites.

Principle of the algorithm

The basic idea is that it is not necessary for every modification to be made under conditions of mutual exclusion that involve all the sites, but that it is sufficient if every copy experiences the same sequence of modifications in such a way that when there are no more changes to be made all the copies will have the same value. Time stamping (cf. Chapter 1) can be used to ensure that all the requests for modification are put in strict order. Each site has a FIFO file f such that $f[j]$ gives the requests broadcast by S_j and

124

not yet fulfilled. With each site S_i is associated a controller that carries out the changes corresponding to the requests listed in these files, with each file taking the elements in order; the controller examines the request at the head of each file and chooses the oldest. The time-stamp on which the ordering is based is the couple ⟨logical clock, site identifier⟩ for each site (cf. Chapter 1, Section 1).

As the requests are not altered during their journey and do not overtake one another the requests in a file $f_i[j]$ at S_i will be in the order in which they were sent out by S_j and therefore those at the head of each $f_i[j]$ will be the oldest sent out by S_j. Thus by examining only the heads of the various files the controller at S_i sees the requests in order. The files must not be empty, for if $f_i[j]$, say, were empty, a request from S_j could be in transit to S_i and might prove to be older than any of those at the heads of the other files. If therefore a file $f_i[j]$ is empty there must be some means of finding whether or not a message is in transit from S_j; for this, S_i sends a message of enquiry to S_j to which S_j responds with an acknowledgement, which, because there is no overtaking, will arrive at S_i after any messages in transit have been received.

The algorithm
The messages are of three types, as follows.

(modif, m, h, i) where m gives the modification, h the time of sending and i is the identifier of the sender; the couple (h,i) is the time-stamp: time + sender

(query, h, i)   the enquiry from S_i to S_j when $f_i[j]$ is empty

(ack, h, j) S_j's acknowledgement of the enquiry

The local clocks are reset at each exchange of messages (cf. Chapter 1 Section 4.2.3) so as to avoid any drift and hence to ensure that the causal time relations (issue always precedes reception) are correctly represented.

Each of the n sites has the following declarations:

variables clock: 0, 1, . . ., ∞   **initialize** 0;
      f : **array** [1, 2, . . ., n] message queues **initialize** ∅;

The behaviour of site S_i and the controller there are as in the following program text; here the functions add and takefirst respectively add an element to the end of a file (queue) and remove the element at beginning, referred to as head.

```
when
a process of Sᵢ wishes to modify the local copy
    do clock:=clock + 1;
        broadcast (modif, m, clock, i) to j∈1, . . ., n    j ≠ i;
        add ((modif, m, clock, i), f[j]);
    end do;
received (modif, m, h, i)
    do clock:=max (clock, h) + 1;
        add ((modif, m, h, j), f[j])
    end do;
received (ack, h, j)
    do clock:=max (clock, h) + 1;
        if f[j] = 0 then add ((ack, h, j), f[j]);
        end if;
    end do;
received (query, h, i)
    do clock:=max clock, h) + 1;
        send (ack, clock, i) to j;
    end do)
while exist non-empty files
    do ⟨(F = {sites j such that f[j] = ∅}) ∀j∈F: send (query, clock, i) to j⟩;
        wait j∈1, . . ., n: f[j] ≠ ∅;
        ⟨j∈1, . . ., n such that ∀k∈1, . . ., n: stamp of (head (f[j]) ≤ stamp of
        (head (f[k]));
        if type of (head (f[j])) = modif then execute modification m;
        end if;
        takefirst (f[j]);
    end do;
```

The operation $\leq$ on the time-stamps is defined as follows:

$$(h_1, i) \leq (h_2, j) \equiv (h_1 < h_2) \text{ or } (h_1 = h_2 \text{ and } i < j)$$

Note that the processing of the acknowledgement messages, after their removal from the corresponding file, could give rise to a new enquiry; this ensures that the requests are treated in the same order at all sites.

Comments on the algorithm
Thanks to the strict order provided by the time-stamping, all the sites deal with the requests in the same order. The query and ack

messages inform the enquiring site S_i whether or not the queried site S_j has sent requests for modifications that have not yet reached S_i.

The algorithm is in fact a minor adaptation of Lamport's mutual exclusion algorithm [LAM 78], the message modif replacing Lamport's request for entry to the critical section and the corresponding release message being omitted; also, since here the sites can issue several requests for modifications, each site now holds a file of requests from each of the others, whereas for the exclusion these files reduce to a single element each (cf. [RAY 86]). If the meaning of modif is changed appropriately and an explicit release message is added, the present algorithm can be used for mutual exclusion without any change in the control.

If the algorithm is to deal with requests for reading, the first thing to note is that this needs to be done only at the site of the process that does the reading. Two attitudes can be taken, according to the requirements of the reading process. If an immediate response is required but the value delivered need not be fully up to date, the reading site S_i must proceed as follows:

```
when received request to read
        do ⟨read the copy; send the value found⟩;
        end do;
```

But if the need is for the up-to-date value, the request must be time-stamped so as to take its place among the whole set of reading and writing requests coming from all the sites, and the process, having executed the reading order, thus remains halted so long as the request is not the oldest. As before, the request need not be broadcast to other sites. S_i now proceeds as follows:

```
when received request to read
        do clock:= clock + 1;
            add (read, clock, i), f[i]);
        end do;
        ⟨text as before with the addition to the penultimate
        line:
        if j = i and type of (head (f[j])) = read then
            carry out read for halted process Sᵢ; end if;⟩
```

2.4 Initializing a new site

Apart from resilience to failures and to loss of data, duplication of data at a number of different sites is all the more important when it can increase the performance of the system; and this can be the case when the number of processes accessing the data for reading (local operations) or writing (global operations, involving all the copies) is only moderate — a situation that arises in connection with databases. There is thus a need for an algorithm that will add a new site to the system and enable it to acquire an up-to-date copy of the set of data.

Attar, Bernstein and Goodman [ATT 84] have provided such an algorithm. It depends on there being an algorithm for concurrency control that co-ordinates the transactions accessing the data so as to ensure that the consistency constraints among them are never violated (cf. Section 1.1). The existence of such an algorithm based on the serialization of the transactions can be assumed [PAP 79], and this ensures that the execution of the transactions in parallel is equivalent to a sequential execution (which latter, by definition, is correct) [ESW 76].

Given the above, setting up a copy of the data at a new site is easily accomplished as follows:

(a) Put a version of the concurrency algorithm at the new site S^*.
(b) Signal the existence of S^* to the other sites, so that they can include this in the list of sites to which information about modifications is broadcast.
(c) At S^* allow a data item to be read only if it has been modified by one of the other sites.

It is easy to implement these activities. Some site can be designated the primary site for any particular data item x; this site, when it is informed of the existence of S^* ((b) above) can cause a copy of the value of x that it then holds to be sent to S^*, thus ensuring that the up to date value is held there and ((c) above) that this is what S^* will read.

The algorithm can be used for recovery after a breakdown, and to create a version of the data for archiving.

3 DISTRIBUTION OF CONTROL ALGORITHMS

3.1 Introduction

The needs for adherence to consistency constraints and resilience to breakdowns have led to many algorithms being developed in the context of centralized databases. As with algorithms for dealing with deadlock these can be put into two main classes. One is the class of optimists, based on the view that conflicts are rare, the algorithms here allowing the transactions to run freely and checking a posteriori for the absence of conflicts that would violate the constraints: if this proves not to be so then transactions are cancelled and restarted later [KUN 81, BOK 84]. The other class is that of the pessimists where the opposite view is taken, and the aim is to avoid from the start any situation that could violate the constraints; various mechanisms can be used to achieve this: the two-phase locks protocol [ESW 76] imposes predicate locks on the data whilst order-oriented protocols use an ordering relation among the transactions derived from time-stamping [BER 81] – the ordering can be partial, replicated, . . . etc. [BER 83].

We have seen that in distributed systems in which the data are duplicated at every site, any modification to any item must be broadcast to all sites. We now show how a total ordering can be constructed for the transactions originating at the various sites; this knowledge enables concurrency control algorithms to be distributed, whatever their nature. We shall see later how to distribute a validation protocol that will ensure that the transactions are treated atomically.

3.2 Construction of a total ordering

To construct a total ordering of the actions that comprise a transaction – **begin**, **read**, **write**, **lock**, **end** – a distributed execution schema based on logical clocks as in [LAM 78] must be used. Here we give the procedure proposed in [TRA 82].

Each site S_i has a local logical clock, $clock_i$, and with each transaction T_k is associated a clock, $trancl_k$, initialized to the value $clock_i$ of the site S_i where T_k originated:

when originated transaction T_k at S_i
    do create (trancl$_i$);
      clock$_i$:= clock$_i$ + 1;
      trancl$_k$:= clock$_i$;
    end do;

The clocks are manipulated as follows:

when at site S_i T_k performs an action on a local object
    do clock$_i$:= clock$_i$ + 1;
      trancl$_k$:= clock$_i$;
    end do;

and we say that the action was performed at the instant clock$_i$.

when at site S_i T_k wishes to perform action A on object O of S
    do send (perform (A,O), clock$_i$, i) **to** S_i;
      wait (done, h, j);
      clock$_i$:= max $(h$, clock$_i)$ + 1;
      trancl$_k$:= clock$_i$;
    end do;

The site S_j then acts as follows:

when S_j receives (perform (A,O), h, i)
    do clock$_i$:= max $(h$, clock$_i)$ + 1;
      ⟨action A on object O⟩;
      clock$_j$:= clock$_i$ + 1;
      send (done, clock$_j$, j);
    end do;

The distributed clock management mechanism is now as follows:

(a) The various actions that make up a transaction T_k are carried out sequentially as required by the text: this results in the changes in trancl$_k$.
(b) If two actions are carried out at the same time S_i the instants at which these take place are defined by the values of clock$_i$; this defines their orders in time.

This enables the actions of the different transactions to be put in strict order: action A_1 performed on site S_i at time h_1 precedes A_2 on site S_j at h_2 if and only if

$$A_1 \rightarrow A_2 \equiv (h_1 < h_2) \text{ or } (h_1 = h_2 \text{ and } i < j)$$

where $A_1 \rightarrow A_2$ means A1 precedes A2.

This ordering preserves the normal causal relations, such as the issuing of a message always preceding its reception, and those concerning a procedural call for an action at a distance [BIR 84]. It enables us on the one hand to prove the equivalence of a distributed concurrency control algorithm and a centralized algorithm, the properties of which are known; and on the other to distribute a centralized algorithm [GAR 82] — for which there is no need to implement the clocks $trancl_k$, which are used only in the proof.

3.3 Distributed atomicity

3.3.1 The atomicity concept

This is an important concept in data manipulation. We must first recall that a transaction is an entity in data manipulation which, operating on data that are consistent initially, leaves them in a consistent state [ESW 76]; and to ensure that the consistency constraints are maintained before and after its execution a transaction must execute 'atomically' — that is completely or not at all. For this, whatever the type of concurrency control used — whether optimist or pessimist — the transaction must use a working space (that is, local memory) and must not modify any data except when it terminates normally, and is not aborted because of a failure, an error or by the concurrency control.

Evidence of the importance of this concept is given in the literature, both for the theory [BES 81] and in practice [HAE 83, BER 81, KOH 81]. Here we mention only its implementation by means of the two-phase validation protocol, as follows.

A transaction T starts by creating a working space into which it puts — and from which it later retrieves — the data it has read. The two-phase protocol is executed when T terminates normally: (a) the values in the working space are copied into the stable memory — 'stable' meaning memory that is not affected by failures of the processes; (b) these values are then copied from the stable memory to the database.

transaction $T(x,y,z, \ldots) =$
begin ⟨creation of working space for x, y, z, ...⟩;
      read (x);   ⟨read data, write to working space⟩
(α)   ...
      write-loc (y, v_1);
      write-loc (z, v_2);
pseudo end ⟨code for T terminated⟩;
         ⟨1st phase: writing to stable memory⟩
         write-stable (y, y_1);
(β) write-stable (z, z_1);
         ⟨2nd phase: writing from stable memory to database⟩
         write-base (y_1, Y);
(γ) write-base (z_1, Z):
      ...

end;

This protocol guarantees atomicity. If no errors occur, the transaction is executed as a whole; if an error occurs in either of the stages (α), (β) it is aborted and no change is made to the database; if an error occurs in stage (γ) the writing to the database can be restarted and will be valid because the transaction, having completed the first phase, has terminated normally and the results have been put in the stable memory.

We now show how this protocol can be distributed when the data are dispersed over a number of sites.

3.3.2 Distribution of the two-phase protocol

Distributing this protocol has the effect of involving all the sites that hold partitions or copies of the data, whether the latter are partitioned or duplicated at the different sites. For the transaction to be executed either in its entirety or not at all, the sites involved must all have the same behaviour, and any failure at stage (α) must cause it to be aborted at every site. Thus the need is for a distributed protocol that deals correctly with stages (β) and (γ).

We assume that each transaction executes at a single site S_i and communicates with the controllers at the other sites in order to read or modify the data under their control. As in the centralized case, a transaction T first creates a working space in which, having obtained the data it needs by a first reading of the database, it reads and writes. When it has completed its calculations, and so reached the stage 'pseudo-end', it starts the first phase of the validation: it sends messages to every site S_j that is involved in its commands for writing to the stable memory and each S_j responds with either 'OK', to say that it has performed the writing successfully, or 'nonOK' to say that it has not; if at least one nonOK message is received at S_i the transaction broadcasts an order to delete all the results from the stable memory, if all the messages are OK it broadcasts an order to accept these results; this constitutes the second phase of the validation.

We must now consider the possibility of site failure. If S_j, involved in T's actions, fails there are two cases to consider according as the data are partitioned or duplicated. In the case of partitioning, the data are no longer consistent and S_j, or the communications system if S_j is inoperative, sends a message nonOK; with duplication a site failure is not fatal to the transaction and S_j can reply 'pseudoOK', which will not compromise the second phase of the validation.

Suppose next that there is a failure at the site S_i where T executes; again there are two cases to consider. If the first phase has not been terminated normally the transaction is aborted; but if the failure occurs during the second phase some sites will have taken account of the results produced by T and some will not. To ensure uniformity, during the first phase a message is broadcast to all the sites concerned listing all these sites, so that at the end of this phase every site will know which sites are concerned. If there is a failure at S_i all the sites S_j will be informed, either by S_i itself or by the communications system, and any site that has received an instruction to take account of results from S_i will broadcast this to the others. A protocol for reliable broadcasting will be entirely adequate here [SCH 84].

The text for the transaction is as follows; to avoid overloading this with detail the reader is referred to Chapter 5 for the algorithm for reliable broadcasting.

transaction $T(x, y, z, \ldots) =$
   begin ⟨creation of working space⟩
       write-loc $(x, x1)$;

. . .
pseudo-end $\langle T$ is virtually terminated$\rangle$
$\qquad$ $\langle$1st phase: writing to stable memory$\rangle$
$\qquad$ **let** $S = \forall j$: S_j is concerned in T's actions
$\qquad\quad$ $j{\in}S$: **send** (write-stable, data concerned) **to** S_j;
$\qquad$ **wait** card(S) responses of type (OK, nonOK, pseudo-OK);
$\qquad$ **if** nbrresp (nonOK) $\geqslant 1$ **then**
$\qquad\quad$ $\forall j{\in}S$: **send** (abort) **to** S_j;
$\qquad\quad$ terminate T;
$\qquad$ **else** $\langle$begin phase 2$\rangle$
$\qquad$ **end if**;
$\qquad$ $\langle$phase 2: confirmation of writing$\rangle$
$\qquad$ $\forall j{\in}S$: **send** (confirm) **to** S_j;
end:

Other algorithms for ensuring atomicity of transactions in a distributed context use the concept of multiversion of a data item as a means for capturing time changes in the data [REE 83, BER 83], and for this they use time-stamping.

REFERENCES

[ALS 76]   ALSBERG, P. A., and DAY, J. D., A Principle for Resilient Sharing of Distributed Resources, *In Proc. 2nd Int. Conf. Soft. Eng.* (Oct. **1976**).

[ATT 84]   ATTAR, R., BERNSTEIN, P. A., and GOODMAN, N., Site Initialization, Recovery and Backup in a Distributed Database System, *IEEE Trans. on SE,* **10**(6) (Nov. 1984), pp. 645–649.

[BER 81]   BERNSTEIN, P. A., and GOODMAN, N., Concurrency Control in Distributed Database Systems, *ACM, Computing Surveys,* **13** (2) (June 1981), pp. 185–201.

[BER 82]   BERNSTEIN, P. A., and GOODMAN, N., A Sophisticate's Introduction to Distributed Database Concurrency Control, *Proc. of the 8th Int. Conf. on VLDB, Mexico* (Sept. **1982**), pp. 62–76.

[BER 83]   BERNSTEIN, P. A., and GOODMAN, N., Multiversion Concurrency Control: Theory and Algorithms, *ACM TODS,* **8**(4) (Dec. 1983), pp. 465–483.

134

[BES 81]   BEST, E., and RANDELL, B., A Formal Method of Atomicity
            in Asynchronous Systems, *Acta Informatica*, **16** (1981), pp.
            93–124.
[BIR 84]   BIRREL, *et al.*, Remote Procedure Call, *ACM TOCS*, **2**(1)
            (Feb. 1984), pp. 39–59.
[BOK 84]   BOKSENBAUM, C., CART, M., FERRIE, J., and PONS, J. F.,
            Le Contrôle de Cohérence dans les Bases de Données
            Réparties, *CRIM*, **17**, Université de Montpellier (Nov.
            1984), 30 p.
[COR 81]   CORNAFION (group name), *Systèmes Informatiques Répartis*,
            Dunod (1981), 368 p.
[ESW 76]   ESWARAN, K. P., GRAY, J. N., LORIE, R. A., and TRAIGER,
            I. L., The Notions of Consistency and Predicate locks in a
            Database System, *Comm. ACM*, **19**(11) (Nov. 1976), pp.
            624–633.
[GAR 82]   GARDARIN, G., and MELKANOFF, M., Concurrency Control
            Principles in Distributed and Centralized Data Bases,
            Rapport de Recherche, **113**, INRIA (Jan. 1982), 91 p.
[GAR 83]   GARDARIN, G., *Bases de données: Les systèmes et leurs
            langages*, Eyrolles (1983), 266 p.
[HAE 83]   HAERDER, T., and REUTER, A., Principles of Transaction
            Oriented Data Base Recovery, *ACM Computing Surveys*,
            15(4) (Dec. 1983) pp. 287–318.
[HER 79]   HERMAN, D., and VERJUS, J. P., An Algorithm for Maintain-
            ing the Consistency of Multiple Copies, *Proc. 1st Conf. on
            Distributed Computing, Huntsville* (Oct. **1979**).
[KOH 81]   KOHLER, W. H., A Survey of Techniques for Synchronization
            and Recovery in Decentralized Computer System, *ACM
            Computing Surveys*, **13**(2) (June 1981), pp. 150–183.
[KUN 81]   KUNG, H. T., and ROBINSON, J. T., On Optimistics Methods
            for Concurrency Control, *ACM TODS*, **6**(2) (June 1981),
            pp. 213–226.
[LAM 78]   LAMPORT, L., Time, Clocks and the Ordering of Events in
            a Distributed System, *Comm. ACM*, **21**(7) (July 1978), pp.
            558–565.
[LEL 78]   LE LANN, G., Algorithms for Distributed Data-Sharing
            Systems Which Use Tickets, *Proc. 3rd Berkeley Workshop
            on Distributed DataBase and Computer Networks*, (Aug.
            1978), pp. 259–272.
[PAP 79]   PAPADIMITRIOU, C. H., Serializability of Concurrent Updates,
            Journal of ACM, **26**(4) (Oct. 1979), pp. 631–653.
[PAR 83]   PARKER *et al.*, Detection of Mutual Inconsistency in Distrib-
            uted Systems, *IEEE Trans. on SE*, **9**(3) (May 1983), pp.
            240–246.

[RAY 86]   RAYNAL, M., *Algorithms for Mutual Exclusion*, MIT Press (1986), 120 p.

[REE 83]   REED, D. P., Implementing Atomic Actions on Decentralized Data, *ACM TOCS*, **1**(1) (Feb. 1983), pp. 3–23.

[SCH 84]   SCHNEIDER, F. D., GRIES, D., and SCHLICHTING, R. D., Fault Tolerant Broadcasts, *Science of Programming*, **4**(1) (1984), pp. 1–15.

[THO 79]   THOMAS, R. H., A Majority Consensus Approach to Concurrency Control for Multiple Copy Database, *ACM TODS*, **4**(2) (June 1979), pp. 180–209.

[TRA 82]   TRAIGER, I. L., GRAY, J., GALTIERI, C. A., and LINDSAY, B. G., Transactions and Consistency in Distributed Database Systems, *ACM TODS*, **7**(3) (Sept. 1982), pp. 323–342.

[ULL 82]   ULLMAN, J. D., *Principles of Database Systems* (2nd edn), Computer Science Press, (1982), 484 p.

7

PROBLEMS OF GAINING CONSENSUS IN THE PRESENCE OF UNCERTAINTIES (OR HOW TO AVOID BYZANTINE QUARRELS)

1 THE PROBLEM OF CONSENSUS

1.1 The problem and its formulation

Many of the algorithms needed in the implementation of distributed systems make use of broadcasting as a basic mechanism for sending an item of information from one process or processor – we shall use the terms interchangeably in what follows – to a number of others. This is done, for example, in order to ensure synchronization in a distributed system [LAM 84] or consistency in updating distributed data [BER 82], to arrive at a consensus in a distributed system [FIS 85] or to manage the transactions that involve a distributed database. Whatever the nature of the network, the problem is trivial if this and all the processors concerned are reliable; if the network itself is based on broadcasting then a primitive instruction is already available, and in a point-to-point network the result is achieved by making whatever despatches and relayings of messages are necessary, as determined by the topology of the communication system. But in the face of unreliabilities the problem is complex and forms one of the central concerns of distributed computation [STR 83]. As defined by Pease, Shostak and Lamport [PEA 80] it is known as the problem of interactive consistency; by Lamport [LAM 82] as Byzantine agreement, or the problem of the Byzantine Generals. Other names are the consensus problem [FIS 85], the unanimity problem [DOL 82], and there are others; we shall refer to it as the consensus problem or the problem of Byzantine agreement.

To give a precise formulation of the problem, consider a network of n processors that can communicate with one another only by means of messages over bidirectional channels. The aim is to ensure reliable broadcasting of messages, meaning that when any processor issues any item of information all other processes in operation receive that item unchanged, or in other words have the same 'perception' of that item. This can be made explicit in the form of a pair of constraints that must be respected in every solution to the problem: that when any process despatches any item of information to the others

C1: all the processes that are operating reliably receive the same item

C2: if the issuing process is operating reliably the item received is identical to the item issued.

Clearly, if the issuing process is reliable then C1 follows from C2 and it is easy to implement a protocol that will respect these constraints; but a process that receives a broadcast item does not know, a priori, whether or not the issuing process is reliable. The difficulty of the problem lies in the types of fault that can occur and the absence of knowledge concerning processes that have failed. Even in the very special case of a network in which all the processes are connected to a bus and so receive the same message, a failure in the bus can violate C1 because some of the operational processes may have received the message whilst others may not. We consider the problem for such a network in Section 4; the rest of the chapter is concerned with more general networks which we assume to be completely connected.

Among the various types of processor failure, the first to be considered is out-of-course halting; this can be either final, with the processor neither issuing further messages nor responding to enquiries from outside, or intermittent, with 'pauses' during which it is out of contact with its environment. With the first type any assumption concerning continued progress by the processes is violated and, provided there is a known upper bound to the transit time of messages between any pair of processes, can be detected by requiring all messages to be acknowledged and timing the interval between issue and receipt of acknowledgement. The second type presents a more difficult problem and for an algorithm that is to be resilient to this type of failure there must be some synchronization between its various components, to ensure that the chronological order of the messages is known correctly. There is also the possibility of what may be called misbehaviour by a faulty processor to be countered: such a processor — not known to be faulty — may send not the same value of an item but different values to different recipients, and perhaps no value to some. Given all these possibilities, no assumptions can be made about processor misbehaviour and the problem is to devise a protocol that will achieve consensus among the processors — that is, respect for the constraints C1, C2 — in spite of this.

1.2 Features of the solutions

Message exchanges, states
For resilience to malfunctioning of the issuing process the constraint C2 requires a protocol that enables the receivers to agree among themselves on the identity of the value received, and for this they must exchange the values they have received. However, as the processes cannot be assumed to be completely reliable, malfunctionings may occur during these exchanges and values may be transmitted that are different from those received. Thus nothing can be concluded from the results of a first round of exchanges: if a reliable process receives in this exchange a value that differs from what it received in the original broadcast it does not know whether it is the issuer or the process concerned in the exchange that is faulty; and equally if it receives two identical values — there is nothing to show that a faulty issuing process has not sent out two different values and a faulty intermediate process has not changed the value that it received. A single round is therefore insufficient and further stages must follow, synchronized so as to counter possible failures, whether complete or intermittent, of some of the processes [FIS 85].

The number of stages of exchanges necessary in order to arrive at a consensus with regard to C1 and C2 is a measure of the time complexity of the solution; another important measure is the cost, in terms of the number of messages that have to be exchanged.

A fundamental parameter

Let t be the maximum number of simultaneously failed processes — either final or intermittent — that the algorithm is required to be resilient to. This is a fundamental characteristic of the algorithm and Dolev and Strong [DOL 83] have shown that every solution will need at least $t+1$ stages of message exchange to arrive at a consensus, which is therefore the measure of the minimum time complexity. Thus the distinction between different solutions rests on the different total numbers of messages they require.

Signed and unsigned messages

As we have shown, one of the difficulties of the problem lies in possible malfunctioning of a process so that it may change the values of items sent to it. The question arises of whether this type of behaviour can be eliminated or, equivalently, can be made detectable by the receiving processes; and the answer is that this can be done if each process can 'sign', unforgeably, every message that it issues [RIV 78]. The signature is added to the message and this and the message are encoded in such a way that the receiver can check the origin and the authenticity and no process can generate the signature of any other; this enables the receiver to detect any modification of the content. Thus a process can detect when a value received has been corrupted by a faulty intermediate process that has relayed it, and so ignore this. The conclusion is that the effects of malfunctioning of processes can be countered by the use of encoding and signatures, and therefore that the only type of failure that need be considered is out-of-course halting, either permanent or intermittent, of processes. In an actual system where there is no intentional malfunctioning of processes — no sabotage, in fact — a simple error-correcting code will suffice in place of the signature mechanism.

The general situation is that the difficulties of the consensus problem arise from the types of failure to which the solution must be resilient and the absence of a priori knowledge concerning these. We shall look at several solutions in this chapter: in Section 2 we consider Lamport's algorithm [LAM 82] in which the idea of message exchange stages is made precise, in Section 3 we consider methods using signed messages, restricting our study to three out of the many solutions that have been proposed, and finally, in Section 4, we return to the problem mentioned previously, that of achieving consensus in a broadcast network.

Note: Schneider, Gries and Schlichting [SCH 84] have given an algorithm for reliable broadcasting that takes account of our two constraints, making only the following assumption: the only type of failure that a process can experience is complete stoppage. This was described in Chapter 5, Section 3.4. The consensus problem has been tackled also in terms of a probabilistic model, in which the processes draw random numbers [CHO 85]: we shall not discuss this here.

2 THE LAMPORT, SHOSTAK AND PEASE ALGORITHM [LAM 82]

2.1 Assumptions

Assumptions concerning the network
We assume that there are n processes among which a maximum of t can be malfunctioning at any one time, and that the environment in which they operate is a reliable communication network, meaning that any operational process can always send a message to any other and the messages are received unchanged in the order in which they were issued. To ensure this reliability in the communications, if there could be up to k simultaneous channel failures there must be at least $k+1$ independent routes between every pair of processes – a redundancy (k-connectivity) that is the price to be paid for guarantee of resilience against such simultaneous failure (cf. Section 2.7). The channels are assumed to be bidirectional, and the network can be represented by a complete graph with n vertices.

Assumptions concerning the messages
We assume that they are not signed, so that a malfunctioning process may modify the contents. The identity of the issuer of a message is known to the receiver — this is easily ensured when the graph of the network is complete. To counter the effects of the complete stopping of any process it must be possible to detect the absence of a message that should have been received, which again is easily achieved: an upper bound (δ) is known for the time to generate and transmit a message and another (ϵ) for the discrepancy between the clocks at the issuing and receiving sites,

these having been synchronized initially; so a message generated at time T by the issuer's clock and transmitted should be received not later than $T+\delta+\epsilon$ by the receiver's clock; if the clocks drift out of synchronization they can be reset by means of algorithms constructed for the purpose [LAM 85]. The consensus algorithm must be known to all the participants at the start, and can be broadcast with the initial values of the variables [STR 83]. In what follows we shall restrict our treatment to the assumption that the processes can conduct a sequence of synchronized information exchanges.

2.2 A criterion for impossibility

Several writers have shown that there is no solution to the problem unless the maximum number t of processes that can be malfunctioning at any one time is strictly less than one-third of the total number n in the network; that is, if the messages are unsigned then $n \geq 3t + 1$ [PEA 80, DOL 82, VAN 85]. The reader can refer to these papers for the general proof, here we shall illustrate the impossibility by considering the case of three processes, one of which is faulty: this example is taken from [LAM 82] and illustrates also the concept of phase and consequently the underlying principle of consensus algorithms.

Let P_0, P_1, P_2 be the three processes with P_0 the initial issuer and P_2 the faulty process. In the first stage P_0 sends a value a to P_1 and P_2 and in the second stage these latter exchange the values they have received; but P_2, being faulty, changes the value to b and sends this to P_1.

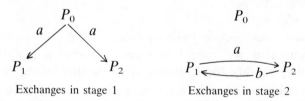

Exchanges in stage 1   Exchanges in stage 2

Thus at the end of stage 2 P_1 has received the values a from P_0 and b from P_2. The second is what P_2 is presumed to have received from P_0 in stage 1 and might modify if it were faulty; if, being faulty, it had not performed the exchange operation required of it in stage 2 then P_1 would have needed to consider some default value, b say. Having received two different values, P_1 knows that there are faulty processes in the system but does not know how many there are, or their identities; and if it is to respect the consensus constraints C1, C2 it must, if it can, choose the value a.

Consider now the same system but with P_0 the faulty process, P_1 and P_2 working reliably. The two stages are now:

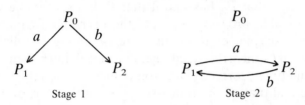

Stage 1   Stage 2

P_1 has the same perception of its environment in this case as before and therefore, having no means of distinguishing between the two, must come to the same conclusion, which is to accept the value a as in the first case. In other words, whatever its environment, if P_1 receives a from the issuer P_0 it must accept this as correct. By the same argument, P_2 will accept as correct the value b it has received from the faulty P_0. Thus the two reliable processes P_1, P_2 have not reached a consensus and the constraint C1 has been violated; so there is no solution when $n = 3$ and $t = 1$.

It is important to realize that in this case nothing is gained by making further exchanges – these can only repeat the results already obtained and so give no new information.

2.3 Underlying principles of the solution

Apart from showing that no solution is possible in the case of three processes of which one is faulty the above example brings out the mechanism used in all solutions – a sequence of stages of synchronized value exchanges; and we have stated that if up to t processes can be faulty then at least $t+1$ such stages are necessary. The first stage consists of the issuer process P_0 sending out the value to be transmitted to each of the other, receiver, processes; in the subsequent stages these values exchange among themselves, as follows. Every process attaches its identifier to every message that it transmits, so a further identifier is added at each stage and the message becomes of the form

$$(\text{value:}v; P_0, P_{i1}, P_{i2}, \ldots, P_{ik})$$

When the process P_i receives such a message it interprets it as follows: at stage j the process P_{ij} has received the message (vale:v; P_0, P_{i1}, P_{i2}, . . ., $P_{i(j-1)}$), it has added its own identifier P_{ij} and sent the message on to the other processes including $P_{i(j+1)}$. The message now says 'P_{ik} says that $P_{i(k-1)}$ has told it that $P_{i(k-2)}$ has told it that . . . that P_{i1} has told it that P_0 has sent it the value v'.

All the reliable processes operate the exchange of messages in this way at each stage; those that are operating unreliably may deliver messages incorrectly, alter them, not deliver them at all or behave sometimes correctly and sometimes incorrectly.

It is essential that all the processes agree at the start on a default value for any action, v_{def} say, to be taken whenever a value is expected but fails to appear; v_{def} must belong to the set of values that can be transmitted.

2.4 The algorithm

We assume the availability of a function *majority* which, given a set of values as its argument, returns the value that occurs most frequently – the majority vote; if no such value exists, the function returns v_{def}.

We consider a set of n processes of which up to t can be faulty at any one time. The algorithm is given in the recursive form of [LAM 82] and [DOL 82], the parameter of the recursion being the value t; we shall call it UM(t), meaning unsigned messages in the context of up to t faulty processes.

The algorithm works according to the principle given above and requires $t+1$ stages of message exchange. At stage 1 the issuing process P_0 sends the value v to the $n-1$ other processes P_1, P_2, . . ., P_{n-1}, adding its own identifier (v; P_0). At stage 2 each of these other processes, P_i for example, regarding itself as the issuer, attaches its identifier to v and sends this couple to the $n-2$ processes P_1, P_2, . . ., P_{i-1}, P_{i+1}, . . ., P_{n-1}. At stage 3 each of these processes, having received $n-1$ messages of the form (v; P_0, P_i), adds its own identifier and sends each message to each of the remaining $n-3$ processes, and so on.

The recursive form of the algorithm removes the necessity for including in any message a statement of the path it has followed, because this is given implicitly in the message itself. Of course, only the reliable processes participate – the others can be acting in any way.

In the following text we give the algorithm in a global form that applies to all the processes; the issuing process is P_0.

Algorithm $UM_n(t)$

> **begin** 1 issuer P_0 sends its value to each of the other $n-1$ processes $P_1, \ldots, P_{n-1}$
>   2 each receiver notes the value received from P_0 or records the default value v_{def} if it has not received anything
>   3 **if** $t > 0$ **then**
>   **begin for** every receiver process P_i
>   3.1 let v_i be the value noted by P_i in stage 2;
> P_i acts as issuer and sends v_i, by UM_{n-1} $(t-1)$ to
>   all $n-2$ processes $P_1, \ldots, P_{i-1}, P_{i+1}, \ldots, P_{n-1}$;
>   3.2 let v_j $(j \neq i)$ be the value received by P_i from P_j
>   at the end of stage 3.2, or v_{def} if nothing is received;
> P_i records the value majority $(v_1, v_2, \ldots, v_{n-1})$;
>   **end**
>   **end if**
> **end**

Example

To show how the algorithm works consider a set of four processes of which at most one can be faulty, that is, $n = 4$, $t = 1$. There are two cases to consider, according as it is the issuer process or one of the others that is faulty. We show the process as a tree, the arcs carrying the values transmitted.

First case: P_3 faulty:

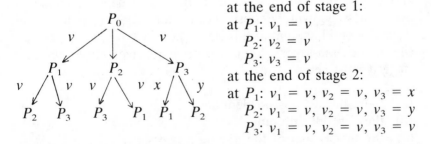

at the end of stage 1:
at P_1: $v_1 = v$
    P_2: $v_2 = v$
    P_3: $v_3 = v$
at the end of stage 2:
at P_1: $v_1 = v$, $v_2 = v$, $v_3 = x$
    P_2: $v_1 = v$, $v_2 = v$, $v_3 = y$
    P_3: $v_1 = v$, $v_2 = v$, $v_3 = v$

When the two stages have been completed each of the two reliable processes has received a set of values and has reached the same decision, thus respecting the constraint C1; and the value sent by P_0 is the majority value, so C2 is respected. The tree for this algorithm, $UM_4(1)$, shows the paths followed by the messages in order.

Second case: P_0 is faulty:

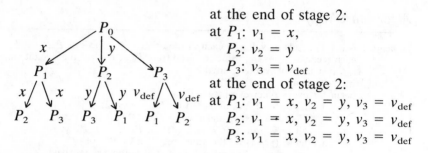

at the end of stage 2:
at P_1: $v_1 = x$,
P_2: $v_2 = y$
P_3: $v_3 = v_{def}$
at the end of stage 2:
at P_1: $v_1 = x$, $v_2 = y$, $v_3 = v_{def}$
P_2: $v_1 = x$, $v_2 = y$, $v_3 = v_{def}$
P_3: $v_1 = x$, $v_2 = y$, $v_3 = v_{def}$

The three reliable processes have now received the same value majority (x, y, v_{def}), and the constraints C1, C2 are respected.

The reader is invited to work through the algorithm for $n = 7$, $t = 2$, taking the two cases of P_0 faulty or not. This will give a better grasp of the principle.

Implementation of the algorithm
The algorithm is given here in an abstract formulation that uses recursion. Implementation is not a trivial matter: large numbers of messages can be circulating during any one stage and it is important that each is identified, so as to avoid ambiguities. Adding to the transmitted value information giving the route it has followed will enable the stage to which it belongs and the recursive call to which it was due to be known exactly (see the tree diagrams above). At the end of stage k, that is, at a depth k in the tree, every message will be postfixed by an ordered sequence of k distinct identifiers, and in this stage there will be $(n-1)(n-2) \ldots (n-k)$ such messages. When a process receives a message in this stage it must check that

(a) there are at most k identifiers,
(b) they are all different,
(c) the first is that of the issuing process P_0,
(d) the last is that of the last process to relay the message: this is possible because of the assumptions made concerning the network (cf. Section 2.1),

(e) its own identifier does not appear in the list.

If all these conditions are fulfilled the message is accepted as valid and can take part in the next stage of the protocol; otherwise it is discarded. A malfunctioning process may corrupt a message by altering the order of the list of identifiers yet still leave a valid message; the invalidity will be detected at a later stage.

Thus in any implementation the messages must consist of two parts: the first concerning the value to be communicated, the second a check field to enable the route it has followed to be known.

2.5 Proof of correctness

Proving that UM(t) works as intended consists in showing that it ensures the broadcasting of a value respecting the constraints C1, C2. In view of the criterion concerning unsigned messages stated in Section 2.2, if a maximum of t processes can be faulty at any one time there must be at least $3t+1$ processes altogether in the system to which an algorithm relates; and we shall show that with these assumptions UM(t) does in fact solve the problem. The proof, like the formulation of the algorithm given above, is based on recursion; we need first a lemma that concerns C2 alone, in which the issuing process is assumed to be fault free, from which a theorem concerning both constraints follows. The proof given here is that of [LAM 82] and [DOL 82].

Lemma
For all values of the integers t and p the algorithm UM(t) respects the constraint C2 provided that the total number n of processes exceeds $2p + t$ and the maximum number of simultaneously faulty processes is p.

The proof is by recursion on t, and there is the underlying assumption that the communication channels are reliable.

The lemma is clearly true for $t=0$, for UM(0) means that all the processes are reliable and therefore C1 holds trivially. Suppose it is true for $t-1$. Then in stage 1 the issuer P_0, which can be assumed to be reliable since we are concerned here only with C2, sends a value v to the $n-1$ other processes. From $n > 2p+t$ we have $n-1 > 2p+t-1$ and we can apply the recurrence: each of the $n-1$

algorithms UM($t-1$) invoked in this stage respects C2, so at the end of the stage will have received the value v from each reliable process P_j, and $v_j = v$ (step 3.2 in the program). Since there are at most p unreliable processes and $n-1 > 2p+t-1 > 2p$, a majority of these $n-1$ processes are reliable ($p < \frac{1}{2}n$) and therefore each of the reliable processes will receive v as the majority value at the end of the stage. Thus the result holds for t, and therefore generally.

Theorem

For positive integers t the algorithm UM(t) respects the constraints C1 and C2 provided that the total number of processes exceeds $3t$ and the maximum number of simultaneously faulty processes is t.

The proof is again by recursion on t. If $t=0$ the theorem holds trivially. Suppose it to hold for $t-1$. There are two cases to consider, according as the issuer P_0 is or is not reliable.

Case 1: P_0 reliable: If $t = p$ the lemma gives the result that with $n > 3p$, UM(t) respects C2; and respect for C1 follows since P_0 is reliable. So the theorem holds for t, and therefore generally.

Case 2: P_0 faulty: There are up to t faulty processes, among which may be P_0; so among the receivers there may be up to $t-1$ faulty processes. From the assumption $n > 3t$ it follows that the total number of processes apart from P_0 exceeds $3t-1$, which is greater than $3(t-1)$. The theorem can therefore be applied to each of the $n-1$ applications of UM($t-1$) of step 3.1 in the program and respects C1 and C2; and at step 3.2 all the reliable processes will have received the same values v_j, for all j, and will therefore have obtained the same value from the application of the majority function. This means that C1 is respected, and again the theorem is proved.

2.6 Complexity of the algorithm

We said in Section 1.2 that there are two important measures of the computational complexity of a consensus protocol, the number of stages of message exchange (which is a measure of its temporal complexity) and the number of messages generated. For the first, we have seen that if there are a maximum of t faulty processors then the number of stages needed is $t+1$; it is shown in [DOL 83] that this is the minimum number of stages needed by any algorithm that solves the problem.

For the number of messages, UM(t), applied to a system of n processes, first causes the issuing of $n-1$ messages, each of which initiates an execution of UM($t-1$); each of these then causes the issuing of $n-2$ messages, each of which initiates an execution of UM($t-2$) . . . until UM(0) is reached. There can thus be up to $(n-1)$ $(n-2)$ . . . $(n-(t+1))$ in all, which is $O(n^{t+1})$. As is clear from the trees of Section 2.4, the number of messages in circulation increases with the successive stages; the next question, what size are these messages?

In the course of the implementation, as noted in Section 2.4, each process adds its identifier to each message it receives before sending it on to the others. At stage k there are thus k identifiers, and as there are $t+1$ stages the number at the end of the algorithm is $t+1$; and as all the identifiers will be of approximately equal length (measured in number of characters) the size of each message is $O(t)$ – that is, it is approximately proportional to the number of faulty processes.

Note finally that in the course of its execution the algorithm UM(t) generates $(n-1)$ $(n-2)$ . . . $(n-k)$ executions of UM($t-k$) at stage k, each of which generates messages containing a sequence of k process identifiers.

2.7 Other assumptions concerning the network

Unreliable network

What can be said about the behaviour of UM(t) if the assumption of network reliability is abandoned? An unreliable channel can lose a message in transit — particularly if the channel is cut — or can corrupt it, meaning alter its content. In general a receiving process has no way of distinguishing between communication faults and faults in the issuing process; so if we have an initially fully-connected network with n processes the algorithm UM(t), where $n > 3t$, must be resilient to a maximum of t faults, whether these arise in the processes or in the channels. Note that the failure of any or all of the channels to which a process is connected is equivalent to a single faulty behaviour, that of the process itself.

150

k-connected network

[DOL 82] includes a study of the case in which the communications network is k-connected, meaning that there are k independent paths between every pair of processes; consequently any issuer can send up to k copies of any value to each receiver, via separate channels. An algorithm analogous to UM(t) is proposed there for solving the consensus problem under the assumptions that, t being the maximum number of faulty processes and/or channels, combined,

(a) the total number of processes is, as before, greater than $3t$,
(b) the connectivity of the network is greater than $2t$.

This means that if faults can arise in any combination of processes and channels, then if there is to be resilience to a maximum of t faults in total there must be at least $3t+1$ processes and at least $2t+1$ independent channels between every pair of processes.

2.8 Other algorithms

The original motivation for the Lamport, Shostak and Pease algorithm just described was provided by the need to develop a fault-tolerant distributed system. Its authors comment that the method of the majority vote, which is their starting point, is not by itself sufficient to give resilience to failures. The method is in fact based on the implied assumption that all the reliable processes, which, redundantly, execute the same program, will give the same results and that a vote on these will give the desired final result. This, however, assumes that they are all given the same input data; so to obtain a majority vote that will lead to a reliable system there must be a means of guaranteeing that the following conditions hold:

D1: all the processes that are operating reliably use the same input data (and produce the same output),
D2: if the unit that provides the input data is operating correctly then all the reliable processes use the same data (and produce the correct result).

We can state that these two conditions are in fact the consensus constraints C1, C2.

Dolev in [DOL 82] gives an algorithm that generalizes the (LAM 82) algorithm to the case of a network which is still reliable but is not completely connected — that is, there is not a direct path between *every* pair of processes. Many other algorithms have been produced to deal with unsigned messages (e.g. [LYN 82, TUR 84]) which reduce the total number of messages needed to reach the consensus at the cost of more exchange stages: the best so far [DOL 85] needs $2t+3$ stages and a number of messages that is $0(nt+t^3)$. We chose the Lamport, Shostak and Pease algorithm for our account here because of its clarity in comparison with the other unsigned message algorithms and because the principles on which it is based are used in other distributed algorithms [LAM 85].

All these algorithms are expensive in terms of computer resources. We have already mentioned the possibility of limiting the types of faulty behaviour considered to cause permanent or temporary stoppage of the processors; we now consider the possibilities for reducing the number of messages.

3 SOLUTIONS USING SIGNED MESSAGES

3.1 Assumptions, importance of signatures

As we said in Section 1.2, the importance of using signed messages is that it enables us to remove the need to consider malfunctioning of a process, leaving halting, either temporary or permanent, as the only type of fault to be considered; this means that there is no corruption of messages, but if, in an actual implementation, corruption does occur this is detected by the receiver. With signed messages simpler algorithms can be designed but the need for at least $t+1$ exchange stages remains — this lower limit applies to all solutions for point-to-point networks [DOL 83].

The network itself is assumed to be fully connected and completely reliable: no communication channel either loses or alters a message or delivers messages out of sequence.

Many algorithms using signed messages have been suggested; here we give only three, of different orders of complexity in terms of the number of messages needed and whose bases on three

152

different approaches to the problem make comparison interesting; as before, we give them in terms of t, the maximum number of simultaneously failing processes, as parameter.

Again as we said in Section 1.2, consensus algorithms using signed messages are of great practical importance when the failures are not intended – that is, when there is no sabotage; in such circumstances the signature mechanism can be replaced by a simple, and less expensive, error detection mechanism.

3.2 The Lamport, Shostak and Pease algorithm [LAM 82]

Principle
This is simple. The issuing process P_0 sends a signed message containing the value v that it wishes to broadcast to all n–1 other processes – if P_0 itself is faulty it may send different, arbitrary, values with different messages; and each receiving process adds its own signature and passes the augmented message on to all those processes that have not already signed it, and so on. When at the $(t+1)$th stage a process receives no further messages it applies the function 'choice' to the set of values it has received so as to obtain the consensus value. As before, the kth stage in this procedure is defined as that stage in which the messages in circulation carry k signatures.

If a faulty process signs a message and afterwards alters it and issues the altered message, this is detected by the receiver, which discards the message; in the interests of clarity we do not give the details of this in the program text.

The algorithm
We give the algorithm as an iteration on the number k of the exchange state reached, when, as stated above, each message carries k signatures; there is nothing to prevent a process from passing to the next stage if it receives no messages at this stage, for the absence will be detected.

Each process P_i is provided with a set V_i, initially empty, in which it records the values it receives and to which it applies the function choice.

Algorithm SM(t) ('signed messages, maximum of t faulty processes')

```
1 Start of stage 1:
      Issuing process P₀ signs the message containing the value and sends it to the
      other n−1 receiver processes.
2 At stage k, 1 ≤ k ≤ t+1:
      when Pᵢ (i ε 1, 2, . . ., n−1) receives a message m containing value v and
      bearing k signatures
            do Vᵢ := Vᵢ value v in the message;
            if k < t+1 then
                begin sign message m;
                        transmit m to all processes that have not yet signed m;
            end
            end if
            end do
3 At end of stage t+1:
      Vi ∈ 1, 2, . . ., n−1: Pᵢ records the value choice (Vᵢ);
```

Proof of correctness

We have to show that for all values of t the algorithm respects the consensus conditions C1, C2. We consider only the case where if n is the total number of processes, $n \geq t+2$. We give the informal proof of [SCH 85].

Consider first C1: if this holds then by implication all the reliable processes assemble the same set of values V_i and therefore obtain the same value as a result of applying the function choice. If P_i is a reliable process which receives a value at stage k, where $k \leq t$, it will record this in its set V_i and the same value will have been received by k processes during the preceding stages, each of which will have recorded this value in its own set V. P_i being reliable will sign the message containing this value and send it to the processes that have not yet received it; so at stage $k+1$ all these processes will have received the value. Consider now a value recorded in V_i at stage $t+1$. The message carrying this will have $t+1$ signatures, and there are at most t faulty processes; therefore a reliable process has received the value at some previous stage k with $k < t+1$; and this process will have sent the value to all those processes that had not yet received it. Thus all the reliable processes have the same set of values at the end of the procedure, so C1 holds.

Proving that C2 holds is a matter of studying the case in which the issuing process is reliable. If it is, it issues a single value v; the receiving processes can neither change this before relaying it to other processes nor construct new values to replace it — any alterations would be detected (and no changes are introduced by the communication channels, as these are assumed to be fault-free). Therefore all the sets V_i contain only the single value v, which proves the theorem.

Complexity

In terms of number of stages this is $t+1$, which as we have seen is the smallest number possible.

In terms of the number of messages, in the first stage each of $n-1$ processes relays a message to each of $n-2$, and so on, so the total for the whole procedure is $(n-1)\,(n-2)\,\ldots\,(n-(t+1))$.

In terms of size of messages, each carries a maximum of $t+1$ signatures in addition to the value broadcast, so the size is $O(t)$.

Thus the complexity is the same as that of $UM(t)$ for unsigned messages, and has therefore not been reduced by the signatures; the advantage their use has brought is replacement of the constraint $n > 3t$ by the much weaker $n \geqslant t+2$.

3.3 The Dolev and Strong algorithm [DOL 83]

Principle

The number of messages required by $UM(t)$ can be a major disadvantage for practical implication, so there is an incentive to find an algorithm of a lower order of complexity in this respect. By restricting the circumstances in which a process has to retransmit a message it has received, Dolev and Strong obtain an algorithm with a lower polynomial order of complexity in terms of the number of messages needed.

This reduction is achieved as follows. First, a process retransmits a message it has received if and only if it has not previously transmitted the value contained in that message; then if the issuing process P_0 is fault-free each of the other processes will receive the same value and will relay it only once to each of the remaining $n-2$. Thus the total number of messages is $(n-1) + (n-1)(n-2)$ – which is $O(n^2)$ rather than the previous $O(n^{t+1})$.

Next, if P_0 is faulty and sends different values to certain processes — possibly a different value to each of the $n-1$ — the receivers will then retransmit as before. If in this exchange a reliable process receives two different values it can conclude that P_0 is faulty (because signed messages cannot be altered) and it will therefore choose a default value, which will be the same for all processes. Thus the total number will be the same as before.

This algorithm, which we shall call DS(*t*), is in fact based on the same principle of value exchanges as SM(*t*), and is an improvement over that algorithm.

The algorithm

Each process P_i is provided with an ordered set V_i, initially empty, in which it records the values it receives in the order of their first arrival.

Algorithm DS(t)

```
1 Start of stage 1:
        Issuing process P₀ signs the message containing the value and sends it to the
        n−1 other processes (P₀ assumed to be functioning correctly)
2 At stage k, 1 ≤ k ≤ t+1;
        when Pᵢ (i ∈ 1, 2, . . ., n−1) receives a message m containing value v
        and bearing k signatures
    do Vᵢ := Vᵢ ∪{value v in the messages};
            if v is one of the two first distinct values received and has
            not already been transmitted by Pᵢ and if k < t+1 then
            begin sign message m;
                    transmit m to all processes that have not yet signed it;
        end;
        end if;
        end do;
3 At end of stage t+1:
        ∀ i∈1, 2, . . ., n−1: if card (Vᵢ) = 1 then Pᵢ records the value in Vᵢ
                    else Pᵢ records v_def
            end if;
```

Comments and proof

The number of stages is again $t+1$. Each process sends at most two messages to each of the others, so the total number of messages involved is at most $2n^2$. The value recorded by a process is either the value v sent out by the issuing process P_0 if this process is fault free (or seen to be so by the fault-free receiving processes), or the agreed default value v_{def} when P_0 is seen to be faulty.

The proof follows the same lines as that given for SM(*t*) in Section 3.2. If P_0 is fault free only the issued value v is recorded in the sets V_i, whilst if it is not then all the reliable processes still arrive at the same decision. The detailed proof can be found in [DOL 83]; the essence is that it can be shown that the first two different values received by a reliable process are received by all such processes, so that if one takes the value v as the consensus values all the others take the same value.

3.4 The Dolev and Reischtug algorithms [DOL 85]

Dolev and Reischtug give five algorithms that guarantee a consensus with signed messages, the aim of which is again to reduce the number of messages exchanged and which they arrive at by considering the trade-off between the number of messages and the number of exchange stages. We give without proof the first of these, which we shall call DR(t).

The assumptions are as follows:

(a) apart from the signatures the messages carry only the values 0 and 1,
(b) the network is of n processors with $n = 2t+1$, partitioned into three subnetworks: the issuing process and two, A and B, each of t processes,
(c) the topology is such that the issuing process is connected directly to every other process and every process of A is connected directly to every process in B, and conversely.

Algorithm DR(t)

```
 1 Start of stage 1:
        Issuing process sends the message containing the value (0 or 1) to
        each of the 2t other processes.
 2 At stage k, 1 ≤ k ≤ t+2:
      when a process in partition A (B) receives a message m
                    if the value in m is 1 and this is the first time 1 has been
                    received
                    then begin sign the message;
                         transmit m to all processes in partition B (A);
                    end;
            end;
        end if;
 3 At end of stage t+2:
        for all processes of A or B:
            if value 1 has been received then record 1 as consensus
                                         else record 0
        end if;
```

The proof for C2 is simple, but for C1 less so. The algorithm requires $t+2$ exchange stages; the issuing process sends out $2t$

messages at the start and each of the $2t$ recipients then sends out t messages, so the total number is $2t + 2t^2$, i.e. $O(t^2)$.

The algorithm applies only to the broadcasting of binary values, but it can be generalized to deal with arbitrary values, for example by representing these in binary [DOL 85]; the complexity in terms of number of messages then becomes a function of the numerical size of the value broadcast. It is interesting from the point of view of its methodology, for which it should be compared with DS(t), and it is of practical importance for broadcasting binary values. We have given it here to illustrate the fact that many different consensus algorithms can be constructed, depending on the assumptions made concerning the values to be broadcast. More generally, other algorithms will depend on what is assumed about the topology of the network, its reliability, the possible types of failure, the possibility of managing the exchange stages, etc. [DOL 82].

The algorithms considered so far have all concerned point-to-point networks. As we indicated in Section 1.1 of this chapter, in the next and final section we consider the situation in which all the processors are connected to a bus.

4 BROADCASTING IN A BUS-CONNECTED SYSTEM

4.1 The problem: assumptions

The introduction of signatures enables malfunctioning of processes – in the sense of faulty transmission of values – to be ignored, and only failure to transmit a message to be considered; but all algorithms need $t+1$ stages of message exchange to be resilient to a maximum of t failing processes. The question arises, could this number be reduced if the nature of the connection were changed from point-to-point to some other form? In a bus system a single basic command can send a value to every process connected to the bus, so the broadcasting is achieved in a single stage. This solves the consensus problem immediately if the bus and all the processes and connections are reliable; if this cannot be assumed we should look for an architecture and an algorithm that will be resilient to failures.

In what follows we shall assume that a value broadcast by any process is received unchanged by all other processes on the bus for which the bus connection is working reliably; thus a process will not receive the value if its connection fails or if there is a failure in the relevant section of the bus itself. Respect for the constraints C1, C2 is therefore dependent on the reliability of the bus and the bus-process connections, and one way to ensure resilience to such failures is to introduce redundancy by replicating the bus and the connections — say, by providing k bus lines, each with an independent connection to every process. This k-redundancy is of course only the equivalent for a bus-connected system of the k-connectivity of a point-to-point system, which gives resilience to $k-1$ simultaneous channel failures. Then if k_1, k_2 are the maximum numbers of failed process connections and bus sections respectively a value $k > k_1 + k_2$ will ensure that there is always at least one reliable connection between any pair of processes [BAB 85].

We shall be concerned with such k-redundant bus systems here, for which the above constraint holds. The architecture is as in the diagram below, with each of the n processes connected to each of the k independent bus lines.

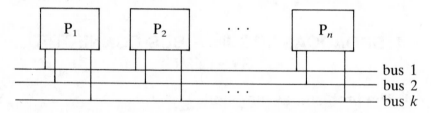

Assuming that the bus system is constructed in sections, a basic command is provided that ensures that a value broadcast by any process is received by all the processes that are reliably connected to the same section as that process; there is no basic command for broadcasting over several buses simultaneously and such a command must be constructed when it is needed.

4.2 The Babaoglu and Drummond algorithm [BAB 85]

Babaoglu and Drummond have given two algorithms for reliable broadcasting in the circumstances just described, of which we shall give the first here; it assumes a reliable bus system and the only process fault to be the inability, either temporary or permanent, of a process or its connections to transmit a value. Thus malfunctioning resulting in corrupting a message is not considered; we have seen that this can be reduced to the case of temporary halting by the use of signed messages.

Principle

There are two stages. The first starts with the k broadcasts of a value by the issuing process, which if it is faulty may send different values on different lines, possibly none on some; it ends with the receptions by the other processes. In the second stage these processes send to each other the values they have received, in such a way that those that have not received anything can make some deduction concerning the value sent.

The algorithm

Let P_1 be the issuing process, v the value it should broadcast if it were reliable and v_{def} the default value taken by the other processes if P_1 is judged to be faulty. Each process P_i is provided with two variables b_1, b_2 where b_j specifies the set of bus lines over which P_i has received identical messages in stage j. The basic command broadcast (v, c) causes the value v to be broadcast over bus number c, the buses being numbered 1 to k. The program text, as follows, gives the algorithm in terms of the two stages.

Algorithm BD

```
1 Stage 1.
      ⟨P₁ broadcasts value c⟩:∀c∈{1,2, . . ., k} broadcast (v, c);
      ⟨P₁ records the value v⟩;
      ⟨Pᵢ (i∈2, 3, . . ., n) receives from 0 to k messages containing v⟩;
2 Stage 2.
      Pᵢ (i∈2, 3, . . ., n) if b₁ ≠ ∅ then
                          begin let x be the value received in stage 1;
                                ∀c∈{1,2,. . ., k} − b₁
                                do broadcast (x, c);
                                end do;
                                record x as consensus value;
                          end;
                          end if;
3 End of stage 2.
      ∀ Pᵢ (i∈ 2, 3, . . ., n) if Pᵢ has not yet recorded a value then
                          if b₂ ≠ ∅ then
                          begin let y be the value received in stage 2;
                                record y as consensus value;
                          end;
                          else record v_def;
                          end if;
                          end if;
```

Comments

If p is the number of faulty processes, the algorithm ensures
reliable broadcasting – that is, respect for the consensus constraints
C1, C2 – if the total number of processes $n > k_1 + p$. For the
proof of this there are four cases to consider:

(a) the issuing process P_1 is reliable,
(b) P_1 is faulty and sends nothing,
(c) P_1 is faulty and a reliable process receives v,
(d) P_1 is faulty and only the faulty processes receive v.

The first two cases are trivial: the consensus values are v and
v_{def} respectively.

For the third, we note first that $k_2 = 0$ since the bus is reliable,
so $k > k_1$; it follows that the consensus value arrived at by the
processes is v.

For the fourth, the number of reliable processes is $n-p$ and
since $n > k_1+p$ this is greater than k_1; so the consensus value is
either v or v_{def}, depending on the conclusions about P_1 reached
by these processes as a result of the information they receive from
the p faulty processes.

A detailed proof is given in [BAB 85].

Complexity

With respect to time, the number of stages is two. With respect
to number of messages, this is $O(nk)$.

The importance of this algorithm is that it shows that certain
architectures can have particular properties that can be used to
advantage for the design of new distributed algorithms.

5 CONCLUSION

The consensus problem has given rise to a voluminous literature
with many algorithms [STR 83]; we have given those that seem
best to illustrate the problems and to provide the most practical
solutions.

The problem is of fundamental importance when there is a need
to build a reliable distributed system from components that cannot

be guaranteed to be reliable. A variant, the problem of 'weak consensus', has been put forward by Lamport [LAM 83] in which the constraint C2 — that if the issuing process is operating reliably then all the reliable receiving processes will agree on the value v received — is replaced by

C2': if all the processes are operating reliably then the consensus value is the value v issued.

This is an example of a practical problem often encountered in the implementation of a distributed system, that of achieving an atomic action in an unreliable environment. A particular case is the validation stage of a transaction that involves a distributed database, the 'Commit' problem [BER 82]; here the effects of a transaction conducted by one particular site, called the principle site, are to be taken account of by the other sites only if these are all operating reliably. A protocol that ensures this can be defined with the aid of solutions of the consensus problem [SCH 85], as follows:

(a) the principal site broadcasts the changes to be made to the data, using a consensus protocol,
(b) on receiving these, each process broadcasts its response 'valid/ invalid', again using a consensus protocol,
(c) after all these responses have been received all sites holding the same data can act in the same way, either implementing the changes or not.

The resulting validation protocol is independent of the type of failure, whether malfunctioning or temporary or permanent stoppage. If more is specified about the failures then more specific algorithms can be constructed; in particular, if the principal site is guaranteed reliable the protocol can be simplified to give the two-phase validation protocol described in [GRA 79].

Apart from its practical importance the consensus problem has a number of interests from the point of view of theory of algorithms. First, it helps in the understanding of certain basic mechanisms that are used in many distributed algorithms, for example the exchange stages that are needed in order to arrive at the consensus: the transfer of information between processes is analogous to the spread of a 'wave of knowledge', enabling each process to add to its own knowledge, and then to spread this augmented knowledge to others. Next, it poses the problem of stating precisely the assumptions made concerning the behaviour of the computing and communications agents: achieving resilience to failures requires the consequences of failures to be specified, and the study of the problem has shown that fault tolerance based on redundancy or the majority vote is only a partial solution which cannot provide a definite answer to the question of reliability. Finally, it has given rise to a number of new algorithmic techniques which can be applied to other problems: for example, some algorithms for synchronization of distributed unreliable clocks [LAM 85] are derived from the Lamport, Shostak and Pease algorithms given in Sections 2 and 3.2.

Thus the problem is a fundamental one, in which can be found models for a number of the problems of distributed computation and control. Its study, and the understanding of the solutions reached, are obligatory for the understanding of many distributed algorithms.

REFERENCES

[BAB 85]   BABAOGLU, O., and DRUMMOND, R., Streets of Byzantium: Networks Architectures for Fast Reliable Broadcasts, *IEEE Trans. on Soft. Eng.*, **11**(6) (June 1985), pp. 546–554.

[BER 82]   BERNSTEIN, P. A., and GOODMAN, N., A Sophisticate's Introduction to Distributed Data Base Concurrency Control, *Proc. of 8th Conf. on VLDB, Mexico* (July **1982**), pp. 62–76.

[CHO 85]   CHOR, B., and COAN, B. A., A Simple and Efficient Randomized Byzantine Agreement Algorithm, *IEEE Trans. on Soft. Eng.*, **11**(6) (June 1985).

[DOL 81]   DOLEV, D., Unanimity in an Unknown and Unreliable Environment, *22nd Symp. on Foundations of CS* (Oct. **1981**), pp. 159–168.

[DOL 82]   DOLEV, D., The Byzantine Generals Strike Again, *Journal of Algorithms*, **3** (1982), pp. 14–30.

[DOL 83]   DOLEV, D., and STRONG, H. R., Authenticated Algorithms for Byzantine Agreement, *SIAM Journal of Computer*, **12**(4) (1983), pp. 656–666.

[DOL 85]   DOLEV, D., and REISCHUK, R., Bounds on Information Exchange for Byzantine Agreement, *Journal of the ACM*, **32**(1) (Jan. 1985), pp. 191–204.

[FIS 85]   FISCHER, M. J., LYNCH, N. A., and PATERSON, M. S., Impossibility of Distributed Consensus with One Faulty Process, *Journal of ACM*, **32**(2) (Apr. 1985), pp. 374–382.

[GRA 79]   GRAY, J., Notes on Data Base Operating System, *LNCS*, **60**, Springer-Verlag (1979), pp. 393–481.

[LAM 82]   LAMPORT, L., SHOSTAK, R., and PEASE, M., The Byzantine Generals Problem, *ACM TOPLAS*, **4**(3) (July 1982), pp. 382–401.

[LAM 83]   LAMPORT, L., The Weak Byzantine Generals Problem, *Journal of ACM*, **30**(3) (July 1983), pp. 668–678.

[LAM 84]   LAMPORT, L., Using Time Instead of Timeout for Fault-Tolerant Distributed Systems, *ACM TOPLAS*, **6**(2) (Apr. 1984), pp. 254–280.

[LAM 85]   LAMPORT, L., and MELLIAR-SMITH, P M., Synchronizing Clocks in the Presence of Faults, *Journal of the ACM*, **32**(1) (Jan. 1985), pp. 52–78.

[LYN 82]   LYNCH, N., FISCHER, M., and FOWLER, R., A Simple and Efficient Byzantine Generals Algorithms, *Proc. 2nd Symp. on Reliable Dist. Soft.* (1982), pp. 46–52.

[PEA 80]   PEASE, M., SHOSTAK, R., and LAMPORT, L., Reaching Agreement in the Presence of Faults, *Journal of the ACM*, **27**(2) (Apr. 1980), pp. 228–234.

[RIV 78]   RIVEST, R. L., SHAMIR, A., and ALDEMAN, L., A Method for Obtaining Digital Signatures and Public-Key Cryptosystems, *Comm. ACM,* **21** (Feb. 1978), pp. 120–126.

[SCH 84]   SCHNEIDER, F. B., GRIES, D., and SCHLICHTING, R. D., Fault-Tolerant Broadcasts, *Science of Computer Programming*, **4** (1984), pp. 1–15.

[SCH 85]   SCHNEIDER, F. B., Paradigms for Distributed Computing, *LNCS*, **190**, Chap. 8 (1985), pp. 431–480.

[STR 83]   STRONG, H. R., and DOLEV, D., Byzantine Agreement, *Proc. of Compcon Spring 1983* (Feb. **1983**), pp. 77–81.

[TUR 84]   TURPIN, R., and COAN, B. A., Extending Binary Agreement to Multivalued Byzantine Agreement, *Inf. Proc. Letters*, **18** (1984), pp. 73–76.

[VAN 85]   VAN GILS, V. G., How to Cope with Faulty Processors, *Inf. Proc. Letters*, **20** (1985), pp. 207–213.